KNOW YOUR INDOOR & HOUSE PLANTS

Distributed by
Horwitz Grahame Pty Ltd,
506 Miller Street, Cammeray, Sydney, Australia 2062.

Copyright © 1990 by Jack Krempin

National Library of Australia Card No. and ISBN 0 7255 2219 4

Printed in Hong Kong by
Excel Graphic Arts Limited

KNOW YOUR INDOOR & HOUSE PLANTS

Jack Krempin

HORWITZ
GRAHAME

FOREWORD

Here in this magnificent book is a complete and comprehensive range of indoor plants to brighten your home. There are 1000 colour photographs which beautifully illustrate the features of each plant and simplify the task of identification. Every entry is also accompanied by text which deals with the basic care of the plant; the type of soil and fertiliser required, the amount of light and water preferred, methods of propagation and a list of pests and possible problems. The reader has all the information required at a glance.

The selection of plants ranges from dainty begonias to large palms, and while many of them are old favourites, others are relatively rare, having been introduced only recently to the Australian market. Each plant has proven suitable for cultivation either indoors in pots or terrariums, or outside in sheltered tubs and baskets. All of them are attractive and will enhance any collection of indoor greenery.

The author's experience with indoor plants spans many years, and in that time he has all too often seen healthy specimens perish through neglect or incorrect care. In this book he demonstrates that building a collection of healthy plants can be quite a simple procedure. It takes only a little time and effort and the rewards are many. *Know Your Indoor & House Plants* will prove a most useful guide in every home where the colour and freshness of thriving indoor plants is appreciated.

Where this book differs from others is in its more comprehensive description of the most-grown and popular varieties. The author, being a practising nurseryman and avid plant collector has been thorough in gathering together a larger range of each plant variety than other authors who only deal with a token one or two from each variety. It thus increases the reference and identification to 1000 recognisable varieties in living, full-colour photographs. For collectors in particular, it gives an idea of what other varieties to look out for. All varieties featured are available in nurseries.

Know Your Indoor & House Plants is of particular value in this regard to collectors of *begonias*, *calatheas*, *crotons*, ferns, *geraniums*, ivies, palms, *hoyas*, *peperomias*, *philodendrons*, *pileas* and *saintpaulias* (African violets) to name a few. Some of the finest collections in the world are listed and photographed in full-colour for the first time. This book is a collector's 'must', as well as being invaluable for the home indoor plant grower.

CONTENTS

INDOOR PLANTS IN THE HOME

Indoor plants have now found their way into every home, from the modest unit to the elaborate mansion. They also appear in many office blocks, providing privacy, deadening noise, and adding a little brightness. They have become a favourite gift for festive occasions, as well as a living gift for those who are sick, a moderately priced present for mum, or for the dad who has built himself a small glasshouse or orchid house. Many plants, however, perish through improper care, primarily because they are treated merely as house ornaments; many people buy a plant just to 'brighten up that dark old corner' or camouflage a disused fireplace.

The nurseries have now adopted the slogan 'Plants for Green Survival'. If you follow the advice in this book, your own green plants should have a better chance of surviving. I have divided indoor plants into two sections: Indoor Flowering Plants and Indoor Foliage Plants. People who look on plants as merely ornaments have probably failed to differentiate between them. My comments may lead to a better understanding of these two classes of plants.

INDOOR FLOWERING PLANTS

These plants are usually sold when they are in flower, and very often are gifts. They include *browallia, begonias, bromeliads,* cacti, *calceolaria, chrysanthemum, cyclamen, crossandra, exacum, gloxinia, kalanchoe,* orchids, *polyanthus, primulas, poinsettias, saintpaulias* (African violets) and *tuberous begonias.*

These plants are rarely successful if grown to flower indoors, but are raised in a glasshouse or bush house where they are brought to flower and then sold. If the conditions in which they are placed in the house suits them, they continue to flower, opening all their buds in succession but producing no more while indoors. When all flowering has finished, they are usually discarded. Those wishing to retain them and trying to rejuvenate them, however, will find it difficult without a bush house. *Chrysanthemum, polyanthus, primulas* and *poinsettias* can be planted in the garden. If no bush house is available, the others would be best on a veranda.

Achimene, aeschynanthus, begonia, bromeliads, columnea, episcia, impatiens, nematanthus and *saintpaulia* will best be grown there. If you feature them in a more prominent position in the home, however, you should return them to their recommended location immediately after flowering or at the first signs of distress.

The modern trend is to treat these flowering pot-plants as a longer-lasting bunch of flowers. With the high cost of cut flowers this is an ecomomically justifiable alternative. The nursery trade growing and marketing the plants use this argument in their advertising. You must be the judge on the economic side and I am sure that should a flowering pot-plant be given good growing conditions in your home, plus the correct care, the economics of a pot-plant will be further extended over a longer period.

Position:
Select a position as near to a window as possible, without the direct rays of the sun falling on the plant. They prefer an airy room to a hot stuffy room. Light and air movement (not draughts) are essential.

Watering:
Flowering pot-plants are thirsty plants and to avoid set-back they should be kept evenly moist and not allowed to droop from excessive drying out or standing in water.

Select a saucer larger than the pot and fill with fine gravel or pebbles. This will serve two purposes:
— keep the plants above excess water level (many people kill their plants by over-watering);
— provide moist, humid air around the plant.

The plant should be regularly watered, not allowed to dry out, and the gravel also kept moist. Some of the waterings may be in the form of a sprinkling outdoors with the hose, or placing under the shower. This helps to retain foliage moisture, as well as cleansing the foliage.

Hints:

- Purchase your plants early in the season, and select plants with many flower buds.

- Feed them with foliar fertilisers (Aquasol, Thrive or Zest), fish emulsion, plant pills, or your favourite plant food, but do **not** over-feed. Follow the directions on the packet.

- Remove any dead flowers before seed is formed, as this will weaken the plant and usually shortens the flowering period.

- If the plant is in a small pot and drying out rather quickly, re-potting into a pot one size larger may be necessary.

- Maintain regular watering and do not allow the plant to dry out at all, as even one spell of drying out may destroy opening buds and decrease further flowering. Alternatively the plant may be spoiled by standing continuously in water over long periods.

INDOOR FOLIAGE PLANTS

Unlike the former, these plants usually give greater permanency indoors, but still are not ornaments, and must be given their correct requirements to survive and flourish. The hardier of these are widely used in offices and public buildings, and require the same attention as in the home. As many of these plants are leased by the proprietors, however, they are often put in unsuitable positions where they deteriorate badly before being replaced. These positions should be avoided in the home. Other factors such as poor light, air conditioning, neglect and over-watering also take their toll.

Most of the plants mentioned in this book have been used indoors, with varying degrees of success. This success is governed by light, atmosphere, temperature, compost, correct watering and correct nutrition. Each of these works in precise balance with the others to produce optimum conditions. If one factor is incorrect it reduces the measure of success. The particular growth instructions in this book may be of assistance.

The following is a list of plants which have proven durable indoors if they receive the proper care. Usually, the more light the better the success of the plant. I have divided this into two sections, differentiating between plants grown just for their foliage, and those which also produce a flower.

Foliage Plants:
Aglaonema, aspidistra, rex begonia, bromeliads, calathea, chlorophythum, cissus, coleus, cordyline, croton, dieffenbachia, dizygotheca, dracaena, fatshedera, fatsia, ficus, fittonia, gynura, hedera (ivy), *maranta, monstera,* palms, *pandanus, peperomia, philodendron, pilea, pothos, rhoeo, sansevieria, saxifraga, setcreasa, syngonium, tolmeia, tradescantia, zebrina,* etc.

Flowering Foliage Plants:
Begonia, anthurium, columnea, episcia, hoya, kaempferia, spathiphyllum, saintpaulia, etc.

Flowering plants usually need more light, even filtered sunlight, so a window-sill position may be best.

Position:
The amount of light a plant receives will be the principal factor in its success. The more light, the longer the life; less light means a shorter life. It is possible to grow plants in darker areas with the aid of fluorescent grow-tubes, the type used in fish tanks. They are most successful, attractive and really brighten up the dark areas. I will deal with this subject further in the section on terrariums.

Watering:
Along with good light, watering is the other major factor determining success or failure. From listening to the problems of others over the years, I have found that most successful indoor gardeners have killed their plants by over-watering. In many cases they did not empty the saucers soon after watering, or tried to make the watering last for a longer period. This can be rectified by filling the saucers with gravel or pebbles as described earlier.

Watering is not a daily routine nor is it a weekly routine. The plants should be regularly checked and only when nearing the dry point should they be watered again. Water meters take the guesswork out of watering. If you do not have a meter, check the surface soil with your fingers before you attempt to water. The small cost of a meter (often about the cost of one plant) can end up saving many valuable plants.

When watering philodendrons or similar creepers growing on totem poles the watering should be concentrated on the pole to keep it damp and encourage growth in this area.

Hints:
• Your indoor plants may be regularly wet with foliar fertiliser or fed as otherwise directed, but only during their growing season.

• Re-pot when neccessary, as indicated by shrinkage of the compost, the appearance of roots out of the pot, or an imbalance between foliage and pot.

• Cleansing of the foliage is necessary to remove dust, which may block the leaf pores or prevent sunlight from reaching the leaves. Dust can also contain plant damaging chemicals from industrial fallout. This can be wiped off with a soft cloth, or rinsed off with an occasional hosing or showering.

• Polishing now and then will improve the appearance of the plant, but oils used in excess can be damaging. If applied regularly, oils should be broken down with water. Milk is a safe substitute, or one of the many leaf shine products available, but beware of permanent shines which block the pores.

• Train your plants into the shapes you desire. Climbers can be trained around ivy ladders and self-attaching varieties occasionally pass back under the soil at the root sections. It may even be desirable to attach a larger ladder behind the first when re-potting a vigorous creeper. Fast-growing plants such as *aluminium* plant or *coleus* should be regularly pinched back at the tips to make them more bushy.

• Plants which become misshapen by stretching towards the light should be moved closer to the light or turned regularly.

• For more difficult positions or poorer light conditions, it may be necessary to rotate those plants with a second or third plant which is closer to the window, giving them time to pick up again before being rotated back.

OUTDOOR SPELLING OF INDOOR PLANTS

The growing position and spelling position of your house plants depends on the climate in which you live. An easy guide to the correct temperature is one where you would feel comfortably warm in light clothing. Some plants may require warmer temperatures, and some cooler. Another essential is shelter from hot sunlight, a must for almost all except cacti and other garden plants suited to your growing climate.

In cooler climatic zones it may be necessary to have some type of shelter house, with or without winter heating, depending on the plants. This may be achieved by adding a fibreglass lean-to to the eastern or northern side of your home, depending on your climate. Alternatively a free-standing glasshouse may be preferred.

In warmer areas shade and shelter may be provided with a similar type of shade-house covered with a shade-cloth or wooden lathes. A misting or sprinkler system may also be necessary to maintain humidity during the warmer daytime temperatures.

In mellow climates where the temperatures are ideal, bush houses can be used as an attractive backdrop to living and dining-room windows. Verandas are an ideal place to spell your indoor plants, but remember that any plant coming out of the house is coming from soft, shaded positions and so will need protection from wind and hot sun until hardened off. A sheltered veranda end could be ideal for this. Do not neglect watering or allow the leaves to burn as you could undo the advantage of the rest period.

OUTDOOR HOUSE PLANTS

Many of today's house plants began their popularity as an outdoor garden or bush house pot-plant before being tried indoors. Some of these originated in warmer, even tropical climates while others came from cooler regions. It is important to know the origin of a plant in order to grow it successfully. This book gives the origin of each variety, and it will be a simple matter to compare that region with your own.

Some plants need full sun, others filtered sun or semi-shade, others do not want any sun at all, so positioning can be tricky when growing these plants outdoors for the first time. Without concise knowledge, it may be best to place new varieties in semi-shaded positions first before moving them into a more sunny position. Alternatively if the plants show signs of burn or excessive yellowing in that position, it may be wise to move them into more shade.

When placing pot-plants the above is simple. When potting them up, never over-pot by potting small plants into a large pot in one go. It is better nursery practice to only move about two sizes larger at a time, allowing the roots to fully net-up the root-ball before re-potting again. This may be further indicated by that plant drying out before the surrounding plants, even though regular waterings were maintained.

Should you be unable to regularly water your outdoor pot-plants you should consider either of two alternatives. Firstly, and perhaps the best, would be the installation of an automatic watering system using black polythene tubing with sprinklers or trickle waterers. The other is the utilisation of moisture-holding components in the potting mixture (e.g. by adding extra peatmoss). Another component may be soaked into an already established pot-plant using one of the new moisture-holding gels. See your nursery about these. I have seen marvellous results lasting for total holiday periods during midsummer with these. I have also heard of very good results of non-drying out when planting in the open garden. One such product is called Wettasoil. There are many others.

It may be best to feed your pot-plants with time-release fertilisers. These are available as three-month, six-month or more periods of release, and should be replaced at that time. Even though the little bubbles of fertiliser may still be visible on the surface of the pot they are probably empty. Additional foliar feeding with a foliar fertiliser through a watering-can will maintain a good appearance.

To make an outdoor selection of potted house plants to suit your various positions, take note of what time of day the sun shines on different areas. This is importantant as morning sun is usually gentle and quickly warms up the area on which it shines after a cool night. Hot midday and afternoon sun is necessary for flowering and sun-loving plants, but tender plants will burn and will need protection. Shade-loving plants may be best on the shady side of the house, but if they are from a warmer climate they may also need to be placed on the warmer side of the home, in the shade and with protection from the wind.

For further assistance refer to the Quick Reference Charts. It is not possible to provide this information on each and every one of the 1000 varieties pictured, but each type of plant will have a reference. It is up to you to decide whether the specific variety you are attempting to place will be suitable for that position or climate in the outdoor setting. As there is a wide-ranging difference between many of those varieties in their local habitat, do not forget to refer to that origin also.

QUICK REFERENCE GUIDE

The following charts will help you with your selection of plants for any specific need. It is important to take into account your own climatic zone. If this is not considered you may damage the plant by placing it in an unsuitable position. The charts have been assessed to suit a moderate climate, such as subtropical or warm temperate, not excessively hot nor excessively cold.

In adapting these recommendations to suit your zone, first refer to the natural habitat of the plant. If its origin is more that two zones different either warmer or cooler, you may have to consider the placing of that plant in a warmer or cooler situation, even if this means a glasshouse or cooler bush house or an under-tree position. Tougher plants may also be happy growing alongside a heat-reflecting wall.

Temperature worries are obviously not such a problem with indoor plants, as most people maintain their homes at comfortable temperatures, even during a cold winter. A comfortable living temperature suits all but the most tender of plants. Perhaps these would be best placed in a warmer room, or one which is warmed by morning sun.

Another method of maintaining tender, warmth- and humidity-loving plants which might otherwise die during winter, is the use of a plastic bag and light bulb to provide heat. This can be achieved by placing these plants in a large tray in the bottom of the plastic bag, large enough to hold all your tender plants in a number of saucers. Place all the plants, the tallest in the centre, arranging the smaller ones around the sides to obtain sufficient light. The bag needs to be held upright. This may be done with stakes or by bending wire into hoops. These are inserted into an outer pot, up and over to the opposite one. Two or three of these should be enough. A light bulb of sufficient wattage to maintain about 25 °C may be hung away from the foliage of the plants and the bag is then tied. This then virtually becomes a terrarium and will require little or no watering. It makes a good cheap-to-operate winter hothouse. Be careful when watering not to wet the electrical equipment and cause shocks or loss of life. It is best to install overload fittings that cut off the power immediately in case of wetting or misadventure.

This method of placing indoor plants in plastic bags, but without the light bulb, is also a good way to maintain indoor plants when going away on holiday for more than two to three weeks. The bags should be placed in a good light situation, but not where the sun will shine on the bag. Close the bag after a normal watering. The moisture retained inside the bag recirculates as an atmosphere for up to a year without the need of re-watering. For certain types of plants the bag should have a small opening to stop rotting.

With outdoor plantings, tender plants may also be protected from cold winds with frames of stakes and side (and in some cases also top) covering. It is best to remove these

	NATURAL HABITAT																							
	EQUATORIAL	TROPICAL	SUBTROPICAL	WARM TEMPERATE	COOL TEMPERATE	COLD TEMPERATE	SMALL GROWTH	MEDIUM GROWTH	CLIMBING GROWTH	FULL SUN OUTDOORS	PART SUN OUTDOORS	SHADE OUTDOORS	HARDY	SEMI-HARDY	TENDER	INDOORS LONG TERM	SHORT TERM INDOORS	HUMID GREENHOUSE	VERANDA	FULL LIGHT	DARK TOLERANT	FLOWER MAIN FEATURE	FOLIAGE MAIN FEATURE	TUBER OR BULB
Acalypha	●	●						●		●				✖	✖		✖	●	●	●		✖	✖	
Acer					●			●		●			●				●		●	●			●	
Achimenes	●	●					●		✳		●	●		●			●	●	●	●		●		●
Aeschynanthus	●	●					●		✳		●			●		✖	✖	●		●		✖	✖	
Aglaonema	●	●					●	●				●		●		●		●	✖	✖	✖		●	
Alocasia	●	●					●	●			●				●		●	●	✖	●			●	●
Anthurium	●	●					●	●			●				●		✖	●	●	●		✖	✖	
Aphelandra		●					●				●				●		✖	●	●	●		●	●	
Araucaria				●				●		●	●	●	●				●		●	●			●	
Ardisia		✖			●		●	●			●	●	●				●		●	●		●		
Asparagus				●	●		●	●	✖	✖	✖	✖	●				●		●	●			●	
Aspidistra				●	●		●	●				●	●			●			●	●	●		●	
Aucuba					●			●			●	●	●				●		●	●			●	
Beaucarnia		●						●		●	●		●			●			●	●			●	
Begonia	✖	✖	✖				●	●			●	●		●	●		●	✖	●	●		✖	✖	
Begonia rex		●					●				●	●			●		●	✖	●	●			●	
Begonia tuberous			●				●				●	●			●		●	●	●	●		●		●
Begonia semperflores		●					●			●	●	●		●	●				●	●		●		
Bonsais							●				●	●		●			●		●	●			●	
Brassaia			●					●		●	●	●	●			●			●	●	●		●	
Bromeliads	●	●	●				●			●	●		●			●	●	✖	●	●		●	●	
Browallia		●					●		✳	●	●		●				●		●	●		●		
Caladium		●					●				●	●			●		●	✖	●	●			●	●
Calceolaria			●				●				●	●		●			●		●	●		●		
Carniverous	●	●					●				●	●			●		●	✖	●	●			●	
Chlorophytum		●					●		✳	●	●	●	●				●	✓	●	●			●	
Ceropegia			●	●			●		✳	●	●		●				●	✓	●	●			●	
Cissus	✖	✖	✖	✖				●	●	●	●	●				✖	✖	✖	✖	●			●	
Clerodendrum		●	●				✖	✖		✖	●			✖	✖				●	●		●		
Codiaeum		●	●				✖	●		●	●		●				●	●	●	●			●	
Coleus		●					●			●	●	●			●		●	✓	●	●			●	
Columnea		●					●		✳		●	●			●		●	●	●	●		●		
Chloranthus			●				●		✳			●		●			●	✓	●	●			●	

Legend:

✳ Spillover plant suiting a hanging basket.

● Applicable for most varieties.

✖ Applicable for lesser number of varieties.

✓ Also suitable.

NATURAL HABITAT

	EQUATORIAL	TROPICAL	SUBTROPICAL	WARM TEMPERATE	COOL TEMPERATE	COLD TEMPERATE	SMALL GROWTH	MEDIUM GROWTH	CLIMBING GROWTH	FULL SUN OUTDOORS	PART SUN OUTDOORS	SHADE OUTDOORS	HARDY	SEMI-HARDY	TENDER	INDOORS LONG TERM	SHORT TERM INDOORS	HUMID GREENHOUSE	VERANDA	FULL LIGHT	DARK TOLERANT	FLOWER MAIN FEATURE	FOLIAGE MAIN FEATURE	TUBER OR BULB
Campelia		●					●				●			●			●	✓		●	●		●	
Cordyline		●					✖	✖		●	●	●	●				●	✓		●	●		●	
Crossandra		●					●				●			●	●		●			●	●	●		
Cyclamen				●			●				●	●			●		●			●	●	●		●
Cycads-Cycas Encephalartos		✖	✖	✖			✖	●		✖	✖		✖	✖			●	✓		●	●		●	
Cycads-others		✖	✖	✖			●	✖		✖	●	✖	✖	✖	✖		●	✓		●	●		●	
Dichorisandra		●	●				✖	✖			✖	✖		✖	✖		●	✓		●	✖	✖	✖	
Dieffenbachia	✖	✖					●	✖		✖	●				●	●	✖	✓		●	●		●	
Dipladenia (Mandevilla)			●					●	●	●				●						●	●	●		
Dizygotheca		●						●			●	●		●			●	✓		●	●		●	
Dorstenia		●					●				●	●		●	●		●	✓		●	●		●	
Dracaena		✖	✖	✖			✖	●		●	●		●	✖	✖	●		✓		●	●		●	
Episcia		●					●		❊		●	●		●			●	✓		●	●	●		
Epipremnum	✖	✖						●	●	●	●	●				●		✓		●	●		●	
Eucharis	●						●				●	●			●		●			●	●	●		
Fatsia					●			●		●	●	●	●				●			●			●	
Ferns	✖	✖	✖	✖	✖	✖	✖	✖	✖		✖	✖	✖	✖	✖		●	✓		●	●		●	
Ficus	✖	✖	✖					●	✖	●	●		●	✖		●	✖	✓		●	●		●	
Fittonia	●	●					●					●			●		●	✓		●	●		●	
Filicium		●						●		●	●			●			●			●	●		●	
Graptophyllum, etc.		●					●			●	●				●		●	✓		●	●		●	
Gynura		●					●		●		●				●		●	✓		●			●	
Haemanthus			●				●			●	●			●	●		●	✓		●	●	●		●
Hedera			✖	●	●	●		●	●	●	●	●	●				●			●	●		●	
Heimerliodendron		●	●	●				●		●	●	●	●				●	✓		●	●		●	
Hemigraphis	●	●					●			●	●	●		●			●	✓		●	●		●	
Hyacinths and other Bulbs							●				●			●	●		●		●	●		●		●
Hoffmania	✖	●					●				●	●			●		●	✓		●	●		●	
Hoya		●	●				✖	●	●	●	●		✖	✖	✖		●	✓		●	●	●	✖	
Hypoestes		●					●				●	●		●			●	✓		●	●		●	
Ipomoea		●						●	●	●				●				✓				●		
Impatiens		●					●				●	●	●	●			●		●	●		●	✖	
Ixora		●					✖	●		●				●			●	✓	●	●		✖	●	

Legend:

✻ Spillover plant suiting a hanging basket.

● Applicable for most varieties.

✖ Applicable for lesser number of varieties.

✓ Also suitable.

	NATURAL HABITAT																							
	EQUATORIAL	TROPICAL	SUBTROPICAL	WARM TEMPERATE	COOL TEMPERATE	COLD TEMPERATE	SMALL GROWTH	MEDIUM GROWTH	CLIMBING GROWTH	FULL SUN OUTDOORS	PART SUN OUTDOORS	SHADE OUTDOORS	HARDY	SEMI-HARDY	TENDER	INDOORS LONG TERM	SHORT TERM INDOORS	HUMID GREENHOUSE	VERANDA	FULL LIGHT	DARK TOLERANT	FLOWER MAIN FEATURE	FOLIAGE MAIN FEATURE	TUBER OR BULB
Jatropha		●					✖	✖		●			●					✓	●	●		✖	✖	
Kaempferia		●					●			●	●		●				●	●	●	●		✖	●	●
Kalanchoe		●					●			●	●		●					●	●	●		✖	✖	
Lamium					●		●		✻	●	●		●				●	✓	●	●			●	
Leea		●						●		●	●		●			●		✓	●	●		✖	✖	
Ligularia			●				●			●	●		●						●	●			●	
Manihot		●						●		●	●		●					✓	●	●			✖	
Maranta & Calathea		●					●			●	●	●	✖	✖		●	✖	✓	●	●			●	
Medinilla		●						●		●	●		●					✓	●	●		●		
Monstera		●						●	●		●	●	●			●		✓	●	●	●	✖	●	
Muehlenbeckia		✖	✖					✖	✖	✖	✖		●				✖	✖	●	●			●	
Nematantus		●					●		✻		●	●	●					●	●	●		●		
Orchids	✖	✖	✖	✖			●		✖	✖	✖	✖		✖	✖		✖	✖	✖	●		●		
Oxalis		✖					●		✖		●	●			●		✖	●	●	●		●	●	
Palms	✖	✖	✖	✖	✖		✖	✖		✖	✖	✖	✖	✖			✖	✖	✖	●			●	
Pandanus		✖	✖				✖	✖		●	●		●				✖	✖	●	●			●	
Pedilanthus		●					●			●	●		●				●	✓	●	●			●	
Pelargonium				●			●		✖	●			●					●	●	●		✖	✖	
Pellionia		●					●		✻			●			●			●	●	●			●	
Peperomia	✖	✖					●		✖			●			●			●	●	✖	●		●	
Perilepta		●					●			●	●	●						●	●	●			●	
Peristrophe		●					●				●			●				●	●	●			●	
Philodendron climbing	✖	✖						●	●	●	●	●	✖	✖	✖	●	✖	✖	●	●	✖		●	
Philodendron non-climbing	✖	✖					✖	✖		✖	✖			✖	✖	✖	✖	●	✖	●	●		●	
Phormium			●	●				●		●			●						●	●			●	
Pilea		●					●			✖	●	●	●				✖	✓	●	●			●	
Piper		●					●		●	●	●				●			●	●	✖			●	
Plectranthus			●				●		✻	●	●	●	●				●	✓	●	●			●	
Portulacaria			●				●			●			●					●	●	●			●	
Primula			●	●			●					●		✖	✖			●	●	●		●		
Poinsettia		●					✖	✖		●	●		●				●	✓	●	●		●		
Polyscias		●					●			●	●	●	●			●	●	✓	●	●			●	
Pseudopanax			●				●			●	●		●			●	●	✓	●	●			●	

Legend:

- ✳ Spillover plant suiting a hanging basket.
- ● Applicable for most varieties.
- ✖ Applicable for lesser number of varieties.
- ✓ Also suitable.

Columns 1–6 (EQUATORIAL through COLD TEMPERATE) fall under **NATURAL HABITAT**.

Plant	EQUATORIAL	TROPICAL	SUBTROPICAL	WARM TEMPERATE	COOL TEMPERATE	COLD TEMPERATE	SMALL GROWTH	MEDIUM GROWTH	CLIMBING GROWTH	FULL SUN OUTDOORS	PART SUN OUTDOORS	SHADE OUTDOORS	HARDY	SEMI-HARDY	TENDER	INDOORS LONG TERM	SHORT TERM INDOORS	HUMID GREENHOUSE	VERANDA	FULL LIGHT	DARK TOLERANT	FLOWER MAIN FEATURE	FOLIAGE MAIN FEATURE	TUBER OR BULB
Rhoeo		●					●			●				●			●	✓	●	●		●	●	
Radermachia		●								●	●			●			●			●	●			●	
Ribbon Grasses				●	●		●			●	●	●	●						●	●		●	●	
Saintpaulia		●					●					●				●	●	●	●	●		●		
Sanchezia		●					●			●	●			●			●			●	●			●	
Sansevieria		●	●				●			●	●	●	●			●	●	✓	●	●	●		●	
Saxifraga			●				●		✳		●	●			●		●	●	●	●		●	●	
Schizanthus *			●	●	●		●			●	●			●						●	●		●		
Senecio			●				●		●	●	●		●				●			●		●	●	
Sinningia		●	●				●		✖		✖			●			●			●		●	✖	
Scindapsis	●	●	●						●		●	●	●				●	✓	●	●	●		●	
Soleirolia				●			●				●	●		●			●	✓		●			●	
Sonerila		●					●								●		●	●		●			●	
Spathiphyllum		●					●	●			●	●	●				●	✓	●	●	✖	●	●	
Succulents		●	●				✖	✖	✖	●	✖		●				●	✓	●	●		✖	●	
Synadenium		●						●		●	●		●				●	✓	●	●			●	
Syngonium		●					●		●	●	●	●				●	●		●	●			●	
Tolmiea				●	●		●							●		●	●		●	●			●	
Trevesia		●						●			●				●		●			●	●			●	
Wandering Jews		●	●	●			●		✳	●	●	●	●			●	●	✓	●	●			●	
Vinca				●	●		●		✳	●				●						●	●			●	
Xanthosma		●					●	●		●					●					●	●			●	
Zygocactus		●	●				●				●	●	●	●			●	✓	●	●		●		

* Same applies to other annual seedlings - Petunias, Pansies, Phlox, Mimulus, Violas, Torenia, Nemesia and even strawberries.

as the plant establishes. Other materials for this use are shade-cloth, hessian, and even sprigs of tree leaves. When planting outdoors, add some potting mix if the garden soil lacks humus or is sandy.

When taking plants from indoors, shade-houses or from shops, they may sunburn unless protected until they acclimatise. Protect them for the first week to retain their appearance. Plants in pots may be held under some protection until a change in the weather offers the opportunity to move them into a more exposed position.

The features referred to in the Quick Reference Guide are the climatic zones, type of growth, outdoor aspect, hardiness, indoor or under-cover aspect, light tolerence and the plant's principal feature. These are all generalisations and specific varieties may differ from the remainder to which the reference applies. Always carry out a second check.

TERRARIUMS

Terrariums may be described as a popular form of art using indoor plants. There are numerous types of containers marketed as terrariums, in both glass and plastic. Some are quite suitable, but most, in my opinion, are very impractical with little or no chance of success. In particular I refer to the dainty glass brandy balloons, small bottles and other containers, which are very nice to look at but because of their small size and shallow shapes are totally unsuited to plant cultivation.

My idea of a practical terrarium ranges from bottles of no smaller capacity than 15 litres to a converted fish tank complete with aquarium light. Better still, with the quick setting powerful glues available these days, an aquarium-shaped, mini-glasshouse with sloping roof can soon be put together. Attach a grow-tube to one side of the roof, and make the other of removable glass for easy planting.

Terrariums are rewarding, as otherwise unsuccessful indoor plants thrive under these conditions. If lit by grow-tubes in a fluorescent holder they will brighten up an otherwise dull corner and create quite a talking point. Smaller arrangements can be made up, and are often sold as gift plants for festive occasions, but in my opinion they can only be maintained by experts. In the hands of an amateur, they would bring disappointment, and turn the grower away from terrariums for all time.

Selection of Plants:
The range of plants suitable for terarriums depends on whether artificial light is to be used, or whether natural light only is available. The range using artificial light is really exciting, and adds colour to otherwise dull places. My illuminated terrarium has renewed my interest in indoor plants, as species which otherwise could only have been grown in my hothouse are now highly successful indoors. A range of plants for growing in terrariums follows.

Artificial Light:
Aglaonema, anthurium, aphelandra, rex begonia, bromeliads, *chlorophytum, calathea* (smaller varieties), *dieffenbachia* (smaller varieties), ferns, *fittonia, gynura, maranta,* small palms, *peperomia, pilea, sansevieria* (small varieties), *saxifraga, saintpaulia, tolmiea, tradescantia* and *zebrina.*

Natural Light:
Rex begonias, bromeliads, *chlorophytum,* ferns, *maranta,* palms, *peperomia, pilea, sansevieria, saxifraga, saintpaulia* (needs a window-sill to flower), *tolmiea, tradescantia* and *zebrina.*

Position:
In selecting these particular plants I do recommend they be grown in a position where the fullest light is available to them, and as close to the glass of the window as possible. Avoid sun shining directly onto the terrarium, as this will build up too much heat inside and possibly 'cook' the plants. Early morning rays should not cause worry. I have one glass sphere indoors in a large macrame hanger against a southern window and between the sweep of the curtains. It is very effective and most successful. At first I used only the hardiest of green plants — *neoregelia, tradescantia, rex begonia* and *peperomia glabella* — and they all grew well. After that I decided to try something more flamboyant and planted a *vriesea,* pink *cryptanthus,* bright *rex begonia, saintpaulia,* and a more colourful *tradescantia.* All have thrived. I kept the *saintpaulia* closest to the window and it soon flowered, so I then rotated the container. Since that time I have had many terrariums, utilising both natural and artificial light, and using plants from the above list with great success.

Bottle terrariums or similar terrariums for table decoration should be grown near a window and only placed in the desired positions when required for display. One is inclined to forget when browsing through favourite house and garden magazines, and seeing plants and terrariums in flattering positions, that they were only placed there for the photograph to be taken.

The best position for the aquarium terrarium would also be close to a window, or perhaps between two windows against the wall. In this position it will receive some available natural light, and draw the extra light required from its fluorescent grow-tube. These lights should be turned on first thing in the morning, and turned off at night, allowing anything up to 16 hours each day, with at least eight hours of darkness at night. The period of brightness may have to be varied for different types of plants. At first I operated mine for 24 hours daily, but the plants grew too vigorously. My *saintpaulia* grew enormous flowers, but exhausted itself in a couple of months. Since then I have cut the light hours back and vary it between eight and 16, according to the time of the year. All are now growing more rationally.

Planting:
There are many opinions on this matter. Some prefer sterilised potting mixes and others have different ideas again. I prefer sphagnum moss. Firstly I place a layer of charcoal in the bottom of the terrarium, followed by a small bed of sphagnum moss. I remove the plants from their pots and allow any soil falling from the roots to do so, without leaving the roots bare. I then place the plants one by one into the terrarium until satisfied with their positioning. More sphagnum moss is then placed around the edges of the terrarium and between the plants until the roots and soil are covered. The moss may be pre-moistened. Try to keep the plantings shallow enough to remain in balance with the container. If you do not like your first planting, take it out and try again until fully satisfied. When completed, take the terrarium outside to water. This should be done with a gentle rose nozzle, which should be finely applied, making sure to cleanse the foliage of the flakes of moss, but not using more moisture than the moss can soak up. After a time, if there is still too much water in the bottom, the excess may be removed by tilting the terrarium to one corner and removing the excess with a drinking straw, siphon tube or syringe. The roots of the plants soon move out into the moss.

Hints:

- Feeding with Aquasol, Zest or fish emulsion is best, but I do not recommend excessive or continual feeding, as this tends to make the plants grow too vigorously.
- Bottles with corks should be kept drier than those without. If excessively wet, leave the corks out for periods, until some of the moisture evaporates.
- If using potting composts in terrariums, the compost must be sterilised before planting by baking in an oven at 70 °C for 30 minutes.
- Use plenty of charcoal in the bottom of the terrarium, as it helps to keep the compost fresh, and reduces the sourness of bad drainage.
- In my closed aquarium terrariums, I find it only necessary to water lightly about twice a year.

POTTING SOILS OR COMPOSTS

In this section reference will be made to the type of soil each plant prefers to be grown in, or potted into. While slight variation from the best-preferred mixture has only slight effect upon the growth of that plant, totally incorrect soils can be most detrimental. This will become particularly evident when drainage is affected, when soil is too acid or alkaline, or when the compost dries out more rapidly than time permits to water.

When selecting a potting compost there are no standards of quality to judge by, even price may not be the final judgement of quality. These days all commercial ready-mixed composts are mixed from waste products, to conserve the natural soils and avoid damage to the environment. They are then made chemically correct and nutrients added by chemical and natural ingredients. They are generally produced consistently similar. Seek recommendations that the one you purchase is worthy, and if satisfied stay with that brand. Some of these manufacturers also produce composts for the commercial nurseries, who pot their entire production in these. I would far sooner use these mixes than an unrecommended shop-selling brand. Should you wish to prepare a mixture, try one of the following mixes.

There is no point becoming too technical or suggesting products that cannot readily be procured; instead I have offered the simple and easy way of obtaining good composts. These days, when everything is packaged, there are many types of pre-mixed potting composts available, and I recommend these be used every time. The most common ones are General Potting Mix, Indoor Potting Mix, Orchid Compost, Peatmoss, and Sphagnum Moss. All are available for sale, in some instances along with composts specially prepared for specific plants. Use these if you can purchase them. If not follow the recipes for my easily prepared mixes, but use a little commonsense with the ingredients I have recommended — they are only a guide. You may have a similar product which can be used instead. If in doubt, make up a trial mix first, use this, and observe the plants for a time before adopting it altogether.

General Potting Mix:

Mixtures of this type are easily obtainable in city areas as potting mix of various brands. These can be used direct from the packet, or mixed as directed with a good type of garden soil. For those who wish it, the following may be found useful:

1 bucket of good garden loam, as used in the vegetable garden;

1 bucket of coarse river sand, salt-free builders' sand may be used but it is a poor substitute;
1 bucket of humus, in the form of peatmoss, vermiculite, leaf mould, compost, sawdust, rice hulls, perlite, or similar humus products, or a mixture of these.
Add 150g dolomite lime, 75g hydrated lime (250g garden lime could be substituted if the separate forms are not available).
Add fertiliser — 225g complete mixture, with trace elements.

An ideal complete fertiliser may be made up as follows:
75g blood and bone, or 35g hoof and horn, or an equivalent amount of another nitrogenous fertiliser;
100g superphosphate;
25g sulphate of potash, or if not obtainable muriate of potash.
Add 25-50g of complete trace elements.

Indoor Potting Mix:

Humus-rich potting soil. It consists of the above mixture of ingredients, with added humus: up to 2 buckets instead of the 1 bucket in the general mixture.

Orchid Compost:

This is also sold around city areas in proprietary packets, but if desired the following mixture may be made up. Plants potted in this mixture should be shaken free of soil each year, and re-potted loosely each spring. In addition, a good liquid manure should be used every 3-4 weeks during the growing season.

1 bucket of good garden compost or finely chopped pinebark and coarse sand mixture;
2 buckets of coarse humus (preferably 1 of peatmoss and 1 of leaf mould) and 1 of fine charcoal (wood shavings and peanut shells are often used in place of leaf mould).
Add the fertiliser and lime mix.
Well-rotted animal manures may be used in place of the fertiliser, but because of the uncertainty of the food value of these I prefer the fertiliser mix.

FERTILISERS

This is a very dangerous subject. Many plants are killed through over-fertilising, fertilising at the wrong time of the growing season, fertilising then forgetting to water sufficiently, or even using an unsuitable fertiliser for that type of plant. Always use fertilisers sparingly; after all, you can always give more in a few weeks, but you cannot revive a dead plant, nor can you restore an over-fertilised plant quickly even with lots of attention.

Fertilisers, or plant foods, fall into many categories. All provide the mineral elements necessary to make the plants look well and grow well, if they are properly balanced in their N.P.K. (nitrogen, phosphate, and potash) values. I prefer to use fertilisers which contain trace elements as well, to give a true mineral balance. Ignore the neighbour who uses this or that, and obtain instead a Complete Plant Food with trace elements from your garden supplier. It may be dry fertiliser, liquid (fish emulsion, etc.), or foliar (Aquasol, Zest, or similar). Each has its particular use, and any one or several may be preferred by the user, either alternately or in a regular pattern.

Dry Plant Food:

A reliable brand of Complete Fertiliser. This is applied to the surface of the soil (at half strength for tender plants). Remember to calculate the dosage at that fraction of what is recommended per square metre: it takes about 30 pots of 20cm size to cover 1 square metre. Water the plants frequently when dry fertiliser is applied.

Liquid Fertiliser:
(Fish emulsion, Maxicrop, etc.) These are watered into the soil. Many nitrogen fertilisers are also applied in this way, but because they are unbalanced, I do not recommend their frequent use. Wash off the foliage after application.

Foliar Fertiliser:
(Zest, Aquasol etc.) These may be watered over the foliage or sprayed on. Observe the recommended strength. Keep the plants out of the sun or they may burn. These may be used as liquid fertilisers also.

Time-Release Fertilisers:
(Osmacote or plant pills). Observe the surface of the plants to see if the small beads of Osmacote are present. Many nurseries use this method. If these are present, wait a few months before applying more, and use a foliar fertiliser until then. Plant pills are pushed under the surface, where they slowly dissolve.

off longer than needed. It may be initial potting of some freshly rooted cuttings or raised seedlings, or potting-on of root-bound pot-plants, just the replenishing of some sunken soil level, or even transferring into a fancier pot. In all cases where potting is to be done it is bad to pot from small pots into large pots in one go. This is bad practice and actually retards the progress of the plant, making the growth slower than if it were done in two stages. The roots should be allowed to fully net-up each pot before re-potting continues.

Initial Potting:
Newly rooted cuttings or seedlings are best potted into the smallest practical-sized pots, usually from 75-100 mm in size. A potting mix, low in fertiliser or naturally stronger animal manures, would be best. If no special potting mix is available, or only a few plants are to be potted, an indoor potting may be diluted down by the addition of extra

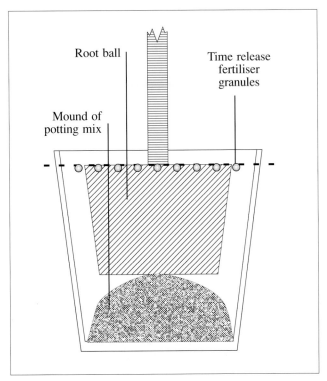

Repotting into a larger pot. Place on mound and fill to dotted line adding time-release fertiliser on the surface.

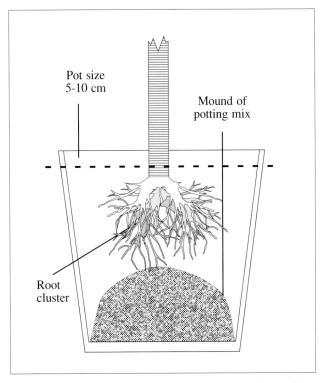

First Potting for newly-rooted young cuttings or seedlings. Fill to dotted line.

Animal Manures:
These are of varying strengths, and are sometimes out of balance. They can induce weeds in the pots, so I prefer to use them in the compost heap, to make a better compost, or in the outside garden as a mulch. The chemicals are more reliably consistent, and not as smelly.

Do not fertilise sick or dying plants, as this will only hasten their end.

POTTING

Potting will become necessary with your house plants for a number of reasons, so it is always advisable to keep some good indoor potting mix on hand, so that the job is not put

peatmoss and sandy loam to about 50 per cent. When potted these plants should be kept sheltered in areas away from hot sun or winds. Weak solutions of liquid foliar fertilisers or liquid manures may be used every 1-2 weeks. Maintain even and regular waterings.

Re-pot larger and into a regular potting mix when the roots have fully netted-up in the small pots.

Re-potting into Larger Pots:
When potting-on advance only 1-2 pot sizes larger each time, advancing larger only when that size root-ball is fully netted-up. After tapping the plant out of the small pot, place this in the centre of the larger pot on sufficient potting mix to level this with the rim of the pot. Fill in

the sides to near the rim level. Give the pot a tap down and the level should lower sufficiently to add a dose of time release fertilizer to the plant surrounds. Top this off with a cover of potting mix, making sure the level still remains low enough for regular ample watering. Then thoroughly water. Refer to the diagrams.

Re-potting into the Same-Sized Pot:
This usually takes place when the soil level has very noticeably dropped and/or further advancement is not desired. It may also be the case where a plant is being transferred from a nursery pot into a similarly sized ornamental one. In the first instance the soil may be wet or cakey. If so, allow the soil to dry out before removing it from the pot.

Tap out the root-ball intact, but allowing any excess to fall away if it wants to. Carefully place the plant aside while you thoroughly wash the pot. Tease off a little more loose soil if it will come away easily. If the root-ball happens to be tightly netted with roots, you have the choice of replacing this back intact, or if a full pot-size, you may wish to remove some of this, by cutting a portion away with a sharp knife. This is easiest done by laying the plant down on its side and cutting the bottom quarter of the root-ball off. This will soon re-grow in the fresh potting mix. Another advantage is that when it is replaced back in the pot it may also be possible to get some fresh potting mix around the sides as well.

Now replace the root-ball back into the pot on top of sufficient mix to level with the rim of the pot. Add the side mix to about full, then tap down the pot and add a dose of time-release fertiliser. Cover this with potting mix to the desired watering level and then thoroughly water.

Should the plant show signs of insect infestation, it is a good opportunity to spray it before taking it back indoors. If not, place it back into its original, or a better-lit position, to further improve. If spraying or placing outdoors for a spell, make sure to select a position where the plant will not be damaged by sun or wind, also somewhere where it can improve without becoming floppy.

Potting into Smaller Pots:
This may be necessary in the case of odd-shaped ornamental pots, or moving into squat pots. Allow the root-ball to dry out before removing the plant. Proceed as described in the previous section.

A variety of clumping habit (*spathiphyllum*, *calathea*, etc.) may also be divided if nicely full, by cutting the clump in halves by a division through the centre of the root-ball using a sharp knife. This will then pot into two pots of either the same size or two of the smaller size.

A single trunk plant cannot be divided, so the root-ball can only be reduced by removing some of it. You must first assess whether this may be safely carried out or too dangerous. One method is as mentioned earlier, another by squeezing and shaking out excess soil. If this is too large to achieve the desired size, you may cut a 'V' out of the side of the root-ball. Shake out enough loose soil to re-form into a circle smaller than the pot-size. Re-pot allowing the fresh potting mix around the edges as well as below the root-ball. Add a dose of time-release fertiliser and thoroughly water. One- or two-weekly applications of foliar fertilisers will retain good appearance.

Re-potting Large Heavy Pots:
If the pots are too large to move outdoors for re-potting, partial re-potting will be necessary. This can be achieved by partial re-potting of one section at a time, over a period of a year or more. To carry this out you require a sharp knife and a trowel. The choice has to be taken to carry this out in two stages or three. If two stages are chosen, the soil with the roots are removed by cutting down two opposite sides to one-third from each edge. To make the job easier and safer it is a good idea to have thoroughly watered the soil beforehand. The holes are then refilled with fresh potting mix. If three stages are chosen, the same procedure is carried out at different times about a year apart on three sides of the pot. If preferred this may be also achieved over four years, by removing one-quarter each time. The best time of doing this re-potting is at the beginning of each growing season to avoid unnecessary distress to the plant.

PROPAGATION

Throughout this book reference is made with each species on the method of reproduction needed for that type of plant. This section deals more fully with those types of reproduction. These are by cutting, by division, or by seeds, as well as by bulb.

Propagation by Cuttings:
The size of the cutting to be grown usually depends on the type of plant to be propagated. Some may be small with soft tips, others larger, with heavier wooded cuttings, from the end of a limb, or even a section from that limb.

Most small indoor plants, such as *fittonia*, *peperomia*, *pileas*, *coleus*, *aeschnanthus*, as a few examples, are grown from a small tip or soft pieces from 4-8 cm long. All of these are easily struck providing they are done in the hotter months and moisture is sprayed to the foliage frequently, over 3-6 weeks. Methods of assuring a humid condition are explained later. The slightly stiffer-wooded plants, such as *begonias* (except *B. rex*), *dieffenbachias*, twining *philodendrons*, *pothos*, smaller *dracaenas* and *cordylines*, *euphorbias*, *leea*, *medinilla*, *pelargoniums*, to name a few examples, are grown from larger-sized cuttings of 10-20 cm. These are planted to half depth, by using a planter-stick to make the hole. Do not push them in, or you will damage the cut end. You may first dip or soak them in a hormone-rooting compound. This may be of assistance for increased root-growth, but nothing can replace constant care.

Some varieties of plants are grown by cutting up the leaf into sections which contain the larger veins. Some of these are *begonia rex*, *peperomia* and *saintpaulia* (you may use a whole or part leaf for these). The leaf sections are then carefully planted as cuttings.

The compost used in propagating should consist of coarse river sand and peatmoss or vermiculite. The mixture can vary according to the time of the year from 50 per cent peatmoss during the warmer and drier summer months to 25 per cent, or even none, in the cooler winter period. It is also influenced by the type of cutting to be struck and the frequency of the watering needed to strike the cutting. I generally prefer a 25 per cent (by volume) peatmoss and 75 per cent coarse sand mixture.

It is important to retain the foliage of the cuttings in perfect condition while striking. This is best done by constant wetting to retain high humidity, or by enclosing the plant with a plastic bag, or inverted glass jar. Nurseries gently heat the compost and supply constant misting of the foliage. This combination is faster and surer. If you do not have these facilities at hand, wet the foliage as many times as practicable each day for the first week or so.

For the amateur propagator the warmer summer months are the surest times for propagating 'soft' cuttings. Harder 'woody' cuttings may also be used in spring, as the weather is approaching the warm-up and growth time. Generally the home grower will obtain the plants he wants from a few cuttings, and he may prefer a few mixed pots of similar cutting-wood types.

Commercial propagation is carried out the year round, by assessing the best times for sales and strike, or if cutting material is limited, whenever this is available. In that case, taller soft tips are often taken from struck cutting as well, to build up numbers more quickly. For this purpose proper heating and misting equipment is desired, otherwise the cuttings cannot be kept on-the-move and making healthy growth.

'Potting-on' is done when the roots are each about 2.5cm long. The first potting should be into small pots to allow the roots to move out to the sides of the pots as soon as possible. Over-potting into pots that are far too large is a bad practice, and only delays the speed of growth in the long run. Re-pot as required, and according to growth period.

To grow healthy cuttings and keep diseases out of the propagation compost a few methods of hygiene should always be observed. Prevention is, many-times-over, better than after-control, or should I say attempted control.

1. Sterilise the compost and store this up off the dirt. Small quantities may be baked for 30 minutes at 82-100 °C, in a domestic oven, then taken out to cool rapidly. Larger or nursery quantities are generally sterilised by steam or chemicals.
2. When taking cuttings, avoid any with dirt contamination, or from the undersides near the soil. Wash in an antiseptic (Dettol, etc.) if in doubt.
3. Only gently water with mains water, after allowing the hose to wash through first, before directing onto the cuttings.
4. Roll up the hose after use, keeping the nozzle off the floor.
5. All propagation pots should be washed with running mains water and sterilised if possible.
6. Think 'operating theatre' hygiene and keep everyone else away from the propagation area, especially the tobacco handlers (smokers).
7. Keep the floor spotless and all cutting equipment and cutting areas clean and free of mess. Sterilise these often.

This set of rules applies to home enthusiasts as well as nurserypeople. Get into the prevention habit and avoid the disastrous after-effects.

Propagation by Division:
Many clumping plants may be divided to increase their numbers. This is best done during the warmer months giving time for the sections to recover and make growth before winter. If small numbers only are required, a thick clump may be halved by slicing the root-ball into two or more sections and re-potting each into the same sized pot as the original. The size difference will hardly be noticed after a month as the plants re-grow into the added potting mix.

Some varieties cannot be handled in this way because of their different habit of growth, perhaps with one main plant and many side suckering smaller plants. With these the plant soil is allowed to dry out before removal from the pot. The root-ball is then carefully pulled apart to retain good-sized sections, or if numbers are needed each section must retain its own root section. Each section is re-potted into an appropriately sized pot, only large enough for its roots. These should each be allowed to net-up before re-potting into larger pots. Liquid foliar fertilisers are useful to retain good foliage appearance. Varieties grown by division include *aglaonema*, *anthurium*, some *begonias*, *brome-*

liads, *calatheas*, *dieffenbachias*, *episcias*, ferns, *marantas*, orchids, some palms, *phormium*, *pilea*, *rhoeo*, *saintpaulia*, *spathiphyllum*, etc.

Propagation by Bulb or Tuber:
This is normally carried out during the dormant period, or just following their shooting away. In the case of *tuberous begonias*, *gloxinias*, *caladiums* and other multiple eyed bulbs, these may be divided at shooting time allowing a few shoots to each section. Allow the cuts to dry out and dust the cuts with sulphur or a fungicide against rot, before planting.

Pots of *achimene* and other members of the *gesneria* family may be full of corms or tuberous roots, when in dormancy. These can be divided and re-potted. At the end of flowering small corms are along the stems. *Clerodendrums* may be grown from root sections.

Alocasias, *eucharis* and *haemanthus* are also grown from

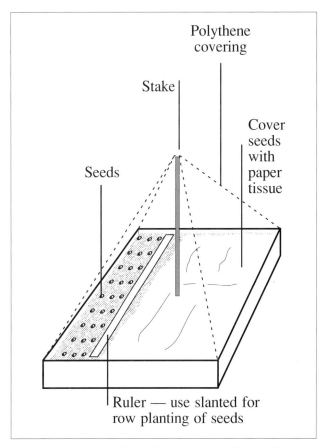

Cover with tent of polythene. Store away from direct sunlight and dirt floors.

the bulbs they produce. I would not suggest division of these unless in their natural habitat, or with qualified knowledge. Try to pollinate for seed increase.

Propagation by Seeds:
This should be kept for varieties that cannot be grown by cutting, or where mass production is required, or where new varieties are sought by hybridisation. Most plants do produce seeds, but many hybridise and do not produce seedlings which

are exactly the same as their parent. Where cuttings are available it can be much more satisfactory and quicker to reproduce in this way. However, some varieties are better produced from seeds and these include *anthuriums, asparagus*, some *begonias*, some *aralia* varieties, *bromeliads* for mass production, cacti, *caladiums, calceolaria, coleus*, cycads, *cyclamen*, ferns, some *ficus, haemanthus, impatiens, jatropha, kalanchoe, leea, monstera*, palms, *pandanus, philodendrons, primula, rhoeo, schizanthus, sinningias, spathiphyllums* and many more.

When raising these make sure to use a fresh seed-raising mix which drains freely and has been sterilised. This foresight can avoid fungal diseases which can attack after, as well as before, germination. Should you wish to sterilise a mix before planting, you may cook this mix, as you would cook a cake, in your domestic oven for about half an hour at about 82-100 °C and plant when cool.

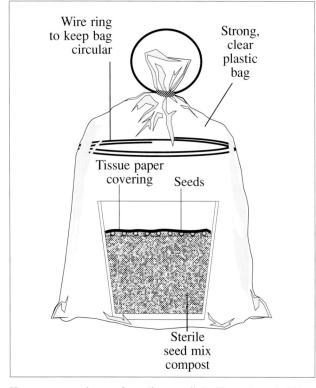

Wire ring to keep bag circular

Strong, clear plastic bag

Tissue paper covering

Seeds

Sterile seed mix compost

Hang up or stand away from direct sunlight. Use stake to hold bag upright if needed.

Place the mix in a hygienically washed container. You may even wish to sterilise the container before planting, but do not place it down on the ground at any time to become re-infected. Water the mix with clean tap water, then evenly sow the seeds over the surface, using clean dry sand as a spreader. Cover the seeds with a paper nasal tissue or toilet paper if the seeds are fine. If the seeds are larger you would be better with a heavier grade of white paper, but not newsprint. Large seeds may be lightly covered or even only half-covered, with the compost, but not deeply or they may rot. The position for growing will have to be determined by the hardiness of the type of seeds being raised. However, it would be unwise to place the container anywhere where it could be infected with diseases splashing up from the soil. Should the variety be a tender or difficult to raise variety, it may be best to raise this in a plastic bag. Sit the container in the base of a plastic bag. Use stakes or a couple of wire-hoops to hold it off the top of the container, then tie up the top of the bag to seal it. No further watering will be required if kept closed. This should be placed in good natural light but out of the sun's rays.

When germinated and the plants are about ½-1cm in height, you may begin watering these every 1-2 weeks with half strength foliar fertilizer. They may be removed from the bag when you think they are strong enough, or should any sign of disease appear. Should the bag show signs of becoming mossy or the surface of the container wet or slimy, leave the bag off for a number of hours each day to dry this out, also turn the bag inside out and keep it washed clean at all times. Should there be problems of disease, attack this right away with the suggested fungicide.

When large enough, usually 1-2cm high, prick the young seedlings into a fresh container of preferably sterile potting mix, to grow on until large enough to pot. Weekly foliar feedings will be helpful.

PESTS AND REMEDIES

Throughout this book, I have endeavoured to identify particular pests which may attack your plants. There are a great number of insects and diseases responsible for plant damage, and in these days of technological advancement, new and better sprays are being introduced to combat them. In order that you may acquire the best product to control these pests, I prefer to make no recommendations, but suggest that you visit your local garden centre or nurseryman, who will advise accordingly.

Scale Insects:
Small hard brown or white insects, which attach themselves to the stems or leaves of the plants, generally ivies, *eranthemums, graptophyllums, fatsias*, etc., and may be dislodged with the fingernail. Spray or wipe over with a soft cloth containing white oil. For the hard-to-dislodge types, an addition of Rogor 40 or Malathion should be made to the mixture.

Aphids:
Need no introduction, and generally can be noticed on the soft new shoots of a plant, often accompanied by ants. Spray with Malathion, Metasystox or Rogor 40.

Red Spider:
These tiny mites gather on the underside of the leaves and around the new shoots of *acalyphas, crotons, cordylines*, etc., sometimes forming fine webs. Spray with a miticide such as Kelthane or Plictran, otherwise Metasystox or Rogor 40.

Mites:
Often not discernible to the eye, and mainly attack *cyclamen* and *saintpaulias*. The symptoms are small bunchy leaves, often taking on a grey or whitish appearance. Spray as for Red Spider.

Mealybugs:
Fluffy white soft-bodied insects, found on most plants, or their roots. They are hard to kill because of the fluff that covers them, although the younger ones are easier. Spray with Malathion or Rogor 40, mixed with white oil (1 part in 100 parts of water).

Grubs and Caterpillars:
These chew out large areas of leaves overnight, and will

attack most types of plants, particularly Coleus, Cyclamen, Aphelandras and Wandering Jews. Spray with DDT, an all-purpose spray, or Carbaryl.

Hoppers:
Chew a long strip out of the leaves of Cordylines and Dracaenas, ruining their appearance. Spray with Dieldrin or an all-purpose spray.

Mildew:
Can ruin the leaves of Rex and Tuberous Begonias. It first appears as white spots, or gives a powdery appearance, later turning brown, and the leaf falls off. Spray with Karathane, or a sulphur spray.

Rust:
Appears as small brown spots on the leaves of Geraniums. Pick off the badly affected leaves, and spray with Zineb.

Drooping and Limpness:
Is generally due to over-watering or under-watering, or too draughty a position. These should be remedied immediately.

Potting Composts:
May be pre-treated, to kill off nematodes, other insects and weed seeds, as well as damp-off fungi, with Carbam (vapam), methyl bromide, or steam treatment.

Over-watering:
The major indoor plant killer. To successfully grow plants indoors, it is necessary to adjust the watering to the balance between light, temperature, location, and soil type. It is not possible to pre-advise any set amount of water required, for correct watering. However, light, airy and warm positions require more water than darker and cooler ones. For the keen indoor plant enthusiast, I strongly advise investing in a moisture meter. This takes the guesswork out of watering, and costs no more than the price of a large indoor plant, but can save its price many times over, in prolonging the life of your valuable plants, and allowing them to grow to perfection.

Grasshoppers chew and strip the leaves

Damage caused by slugs and snails

Aphis suck and disfigure new shoots and foliage

Mites on the underside of Croton leaves

Caterpillars roll, chew, and strip palm leaves

Mealy bugs are protected by a waxy fluff coating

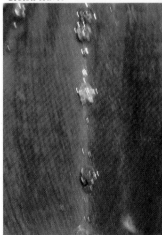

Pink scale is more difficult to control than softer scales

11

ACALYPHA
Euphorbiaceae
Fijian Fire Plants, Chenille Plants

Colourful range of tropical foliage plants with tassel-like flowers. The species vary from outdoor garden shrubs to pot plants for glasshouses, indoor sunrooms, or patios.

Grow: In tropical garden, warm bush-house, or glasshouse. Filtered to bright sun.

Position indoors: Sunroom or near bright window. Remove outdoors or to glasshouse at first signs of distress.

Soil: General Potting Mix.

Water: Soak thoroughly when dry.

Fertiliser: Complete Plant Food (dry, liquid, or foliar) every month.

Propagation: By cuttings.

Pests and problems: Watch for spider mites.

Varieties include:

A. hispida (sanderi) Chenille Plant (India). Bright green hairy leaves, and pinkish-red tassel flowers hanging down.

A. hispida **'Rubra'** (India). Similar to above but with bronzy-green foliage and deeper red tassel flowers.

A. wilkesiana **bronze hybrid*.** The deeply toothed rich bronze leaves are heavily fluted.

A. wilkesiana **margined hybrid*.** Of similar form to the above, but the rich green leaves are margined with deep cream and yellow.

A. wilkesiana macafeana (New Hebrides). A branching shrub, with oval red leaves, marbled crimson and bronze.

A. wilkesiana **obovata*** (Polynesia). A branching variety with large notched mid-green leaves, edged creamy-white.

A. wilkesiana **'Rose Glow'.** Leaves are brilliantly mottled in rosy red to bronzy red. Compact growth.

A. wilkesiana **'Sunset Hue'.** Bright yellow to rosy pink.

A. wilkesiana **'Thai Kamyok'.** This variety has multi-coloured leaf variegation.

*Throughout the book, all entries marked with an asterisk are not illustrated.

Acalypha hispida, Chenille Plant

Acalypha wilkesiana 'Macafeana'

Acalypha wilkesiana 'Thai Kamyok'

Acalypha hispida 'Rubra', Red Chenille Plant

12

ACER   Aceraceae

Japanese Maple

A colourful deciduous tree grown outdoors, but occasionally used as an indoor or bonsai specimen.

Grow: Cool outdoor garden or large pot.
Position indoors: Sunroom or bright airy window.
Soil: General Potting Mix.
Water: On dry side, but thoroughly soak when dry.
Fertiliser: Complete Plant Food, monthly, during growth period.
Propagation: By seeds, cuttings, or layering; use choicer varieties.
Pests and problems: None in particular.

Varieties include:
A. palmatum (Japan, Korea). Japanese Maple. Spring foliage from red to green, turning to brilliant red for autumn. There are many choicer variants now available, with more colour, and dissected foliage.

Acalypha wilkesiana 'Sunset Hue'

Acer palmatum, Japanese Maple

Acalypha wilkesiana 'Rose Glow'

13

ACHIMENES

Gesneriaceae

Magic Flowers

Small, trailing plants, for hanging baskets or pots, which bear colourful flowers during the summer months. Winter dormant.

Grow: In glasshouse or warm bush-house.

Position indoors: Bright light to filtered sun, in sunroom or near bright window.

Soil: Indoor Potting Mix.

Water: Keep moist during growth, and dry when dormant.

Fertiliser: Complete Plant Food (liquid or foliar) monthly, until flowering ceases, then none.

Propagation: After flowering, collect the small rhizomes from along the dying stems, or when dormant knock out the pots and divide the number of rhizomes for repotting in spring.

Pests and problems: None in particular.

Varieties include:

A. longiflora* (Mexico, Guatemala). A tall-growing, slender-stemmed, bulbous plant, resting in winter, and producing violet-blue flowers. An ideal plant for fern baskets.

A. longiflora **double purple.** Double mauve-purple flowers with silver reverse.

A. longiflora **red and gold.** Red bell, with gold netted throat.

A. longiflora **single mauve.** Single mauve flowers.

A. longiflora **single red.** Many small single scarlet flowers.

A. longiflora **single purple.** Single purple flowers.

Achimenes sp., Single Mauve

Achimenes sp., Double Purple.

Achimenes sp., Single Purple

Achimenes sp., Red and Gold

Achimenes sp., Single Red

AESCHYNANTHUS   Gesneriaceae

Lipstick Plants

Attractive trailer for hanging pots or baskets, for glasshouse, bush-house, sunroom, or near bright window indoors.

Grow: In sheltered, warm bush-houses or glasshouses.
Position indoors: Bright light to filtered sun in sunroom or near well-lit window.
Soil: Indoor Potting Mix.
Water: Keep moist but not over-wet.
Fertiliser: Complete Plant Food (liquid or foliar) monthly.
Propagation: By cuttings.
Pests and problems: None in particular.

Varieties include:
A. sp. × **'Black Pagoda'.** A beautiful variety, with the foliage of *'marmorata'* and the orange to red flower of *'speciosa'* freely produced.
A. bracteatus. A short-stemmed trailer, for baskets, with deep green leaves, and scarlet tongue flowers in black-purple tube.
A. marmoratus (zebrinus) (Thailand). The Zebra Basket Vine. A thickly hanging variety, with dark green leaves, banded yellow and maroon, and maroon beneath. Green flowers.
A. radicans (lobbianus) (Java). Lipstick Plant . A short-stemmed basket trailer, with small deep-green leaves, and vivid-red flowers in a black outer tube.
A. speciosus (Java). A short trailer, with stems to 60 cm and waxy green leaves; clusters of attractive orange, yellow, and red tubular flowers.

Aeschynanthus × 'Black Pagoda'

Aeschynanthus radicans (lobbyanus), Lipstick Plant

Aeschynanthus bracteatus

Aeschynanthus marmoratus, Zebra Basket Vine

Aeschynanthus speciosus

AGLAONEMA   Araceae

Chinese Evergreens

Highly prized tropical plants which are very adaptable for both indoors and greenhouse use. They bear a resemblance to Dieffenbachias, to which they are related.

Grow: In glasshouse or bush-house, in filtered sun to good light.
Position indoors: Best grown in good light in sunroom, but will tolerate medium light position indoors.
Water: Keep moist (not over-wet) in summer, drier in winter. Cut stems can be grown in water only.
Soil: Indoor Potting Mix.
Fertiliser: Complete Plant Food every few months, foliar (Aquasol) every 3–4 weeks during summer.
Propagation: From cuttings and seeds.
Pests and problems: Very few.

Varieties include:
A. commutatum (Malaya). Green leaf with silvery-grey markings, and berries after lily-flowers.
A. commutatum **'Pseudo-bracteatum'** (Malaya). Golden Evergreen. A colourful variety with deep-green leaves variegated light green, yellow, and creamy white; stems white marbled green.
A. commutatum **'Pseudo-bracteatum'** White Rajah. This is a beautiful cream and white sport.
A. commutatum **'Treubii'** (Celebes). Narrow blue-green leaves attractively marked with silvery-grey.
A. crispum **(roebellini)** (Malaya, Borneo). Showy grey-green leaves marked with silvery-grey.
A. costatum foxii (Malaya). Spotted Evergreen. Short plant, leaves have a white centre stripe and spots.
A. hospitum* (Thailand). Deep-green glossy, oval leaves, spotted white on wiry stem.
A. marantifolium (Moluccas). Deep-green leaves with silvery feathering, on pinkish stems.
A. modestum (China). Chinese Evergreen. Dark-green ribbed leaf on cane-like stems; berries after lily flowers. Long-lasting and hardiest variety, even in dark situations, and long lasting indoors.
A. nitidum **Curtisii** (*oblongifolium* **Curtisii**) (Malaya). Bluish-green leaves marked with a silvery feather design.
A. **'Parrot Jungle'.** Narrow leaves, broader than 'Treubii', in deep green and silver.
A. **'Silver King'.** Striking variety with suckering habit, leaves almost silver-grey.
A. **'Silver Queen'.** Similar to, but leaves narrower than, 'Silver King'.
A. **'Malay Beauty'** (Malaya). Has glossy black-green leaves, with vivid silver flecks. Also called 'Pewter'.

HOMALOMENA
Silver Shield

H. wallisii (Colombia). Low plant resembling an Aglaonema, and requiring similar treatment. It has deep green leaves, overlaid in yellow to silver.

Aglaonema commutatum

Aglaonema commutatum 'Pseudo-bracteatum', Golden Evergreen

Aglaonema crispum (roebellini)

Aglaonema costatum foxii, Spotted Evergreen

Aglaonema 'Parrot Jungle'

Aglaonema commutatum
'Pseudo-bracteatum', White Rajah

Aglaonema commutatum 'Treubii'

Aglaonema marantifolium

Aglaonema 'Silver King'

Aglaonema modestum, Chinese
Evergreen

Aglaonema 'Malay Beauty'
or 'Pewter'.

Aglaonema nitidum 'Curtisii'

Aglaonema 'Silver Queen'

Homalomena wallisii

ALOCASIA   Araceae

Elephants' Ears

Vividly veined tropical plants, which add that touch of class in your glasshouse or sunroom. Dormant winter bulb.

Grow: In warm glasshouse or tropical bush-house, during the hotter months.
Position indoors: Warm sunroom, filtered sun to bright light.
Water: Keep moist during growth, lay pot on side for dormancy.
Soil: Indoor Potting Mix.
Fertiliser: Complete Plant Food when re-potting, foliar (Aquasol) every 3–4 weeks during growth.
Propagation: By bulb multiplication (tropical).
Pests and problems: Watch for spider mite. Keep warm.

Varieties include:
A. amazonica. Very deep green, scalloped leaves, with contrasting white veins and margins.
A. sp. × chantriei. Deep olive green, with silver and white veins and margins.
A. cucullata (Bengal, Burma). Smaller, spoon-shaped, deep-green leaves with prominent veins.
A. cuprea (Borneo). Large, oval, metallic-green leaves with deeply depressed veins; leaf purple beneath.
A. indica metallica (Malaya). Deep olive-green leaves with metallic overcoat; underside and stems purple; veins are prominent.
A. korthalsii (thibautiana)* (Borneo). Greyish-green leaves, with silver veining. Purple beneath.
A. longiloba (Java). Bluish-green, arrow-shaped leaf, veined and margined silver-grey.
A. lowii grandis* (Malaya). An attractive variety with metallic bluish-green leaves, purple beneath, grey margins and silver veins.
A. macrorhiza 'Variegata' (East Indies). A very striking plant with large light-green leaves, blotched white.
A. portei* (New Guinea, Philippines). Large, deeply lobed green leaves on brown, mottled stems.
A. sanderiana (Philippines). Long metallic-green leaves, deeply lobed, prominent white ribs, purple reverse.
A. sedenii. Deep metallic-green leaves, with raised grey margins. Purple beneath.
A. watsoniana (Sumatra). Large blue-green leaf with silver-white margins and veins, purple beneath.

COLOCASIA

These tuberous tropical plants are usually to be found in the hands of the plant collector. Closely related to Caladiums and Alocasias.

C. antiquorum illustris (East Indies). The Black Caladium. Smallish heart-shaped dull-green leaves, with black-purple blotches between the veins.
C. marshallii. Smallish heart-shaped thin deep-green leaves with creamy-white variegations.

Alocasia amazonica

Alocasia sedenii

Alocasia macrorhiza 'Variegata'

Alocasia × chantriei

Alocasia cucullata

Alocasia cuprea

Alocasia indica metallica

Alocasia longiloba

Colocasia antiquorum illustris, Black Caladium

Alocasia sanderiana

Alocasia watsoniana

Colocasia marshallii

19

ANTHURIUM Araceae

Wax Flowers

These much-prized plants, so often linked with Hawaii, can be grown quite successfully in the home, as well as in the greenhouse. Flowers keep for 4–6 weeks, and are often seen in spectacular floral displays.

Grow: In cool to warm glasshouse or sunroom, or in the tropics, in a shady bush-house.
Position indoors: Shady sunroom, or near a well-lit window.
Water: Preferably immerse the pot in water for a few minutes, once or twice weekly.
Soil: Orchid Compost, or a suitable coarse fast-draining compost.
Fertiliser: Complete Plant Food every 2–3 months, foliar (Aquasol) every month.
Propagation: From seeds or divide clustered plants.
Pests and problems: Watch for aphis, or caterpillars. Don't leave excess water in saucers. Remove outdoors if showing distress.

Varieties include:
A. andreanum (Colombia). Hawaiian Lily or Palette Flower. Green heart-shaped leaves and showy red, pink, white, orange, or bi-colour lily-like flowers, yellow tongue. Flowers last for months.
A. clavigerum (Colombia, Peru). A tall robust variety, with large, heavy textured flowers, in bright pink.
A. crystalinum (Colombia). Large striking heart-shaped velvety-green leaves with white veins; flower insignificant, green.
A. scherzerianum (Costa Rica). Flamingo Flower. Tough narrow leaves; scarlet, pink or white lily-like waxy flowers with a yellow tongue, which last for months.
A. scherzerianum rothschildianum. Beautifully spotted flowers of white on red or reverse.
A. veitchii (Colombia). King Anthurium. The long quilted leaves are quite spectacular.
*A. warocqueanum** (Colombia). Queen Anthurium. A slow-climbing species with showy, long tapering, velvety, deep-green leaves with ivory veins.

Anthurium crystalinum

Anthurium scherzerianum rothschildianum

Anthurium clavigerum, Hooded Anthurium

Anthurium andreanum 'White Bicolour'

Anthurium andreanum 'Red Bicolour'

Anthurium andreanum 'Hawaiian Lily',
Palette Flower

Anthurium veitchii, King Anthurium

Anthurium scherzerianum, Flamingo Flower

APHELANDRA   Acanthaceae
Zebra Plant

The striking foliage, and rich yellow to red flowers of this plant attract all who see it. Widely used indoors, or in terrariums.

Grow: In warm glasshouse or sunroom.
Position indoors: Requires filtered sun to warm bright light, in sunroom or near window indoors.
Water: Keep evenly moist.
Soil: Indoor Potting Mix.
Fertiliser: Complete Plant Food every 2 months, foliar (Aquasol) monthly.
Propagation: From cuttings.
Pests and problems: None in particular.

Varieties include:
A. aurantiaca roezlii (Mexico). Deep-green leaves, silvery-grey between the veins; orange-scarlet flowers.
A. chamissoniana* (Brazil). An erect grower with thinner green leaves, variegated silver-white between the veins; yellow bract and flowers.
A. squarrosa **'Louisae'** (Brazil). Handsome green leaves with prominent white veins; yellow flowers in autumn.
A. squarrosa **'Apollo'** (similar to 'White Cloud'). Green leaves heavily marked and veined in white.
A. squarrosa **'Red Apollo'** (similar to 'Red Cloud'). As above with red tinge.
A. squarrosa **'Dania'**. A more stocky variety, with the glossy deep green leaves more vividly marked white; yellow flower head.
A. squarrosa **'Florida Beauty'**. The most vividly marked variety, some leaves almost completely white; yellow flower head.

Aphelandra squarrosa 'Apollo', White Cloud

Aphelandra squarrosa 'Florida Beauty'

Aphelandra squarrosa 'Dania'

Aphelandra squarrosa 'Louisae', Zebra Plant

Aphelandra aurantiaca roezlii, Fiery Spike

Aphelandra squarossa 'Red Apollo', Red Cloud

THE ARALIAS — Araliaceae

Dizygotheca, Fatsia, Polyscias and Trevesia

DIZYGOTHECA
False Aralia

This unusual small plant, often called Aralia, is becoming more and more popular, both for indoors and outdoors, where it becomes an interesting poolside subject, growing to about 2 m. The foliage broadens and turns green, and bears no resemblance to the juvenile form, which is narrow-leafed and slender.

Grow: In glasshouse or warm bush-house. Outdoors in temperate areas, in sheltered positions.
Position indoors: In sunroom or near bright, warm, airy window. Multiple planting or pinching back produces a fuller pot.
Water: Keep evenly moist, preferably immerse pot.
Soil: General Potting Mix.
Fertiliser: Complete Plant Food monthly, or alternate with foliar.
Propagation: From seed or cuttings.
Pests and problems: Watch for spider mites.

Varieties include:
D. elegantissima (New Hebrides). A slender palm-like plant with narrow-lobed bronzy leaves on a cream, mottled stem.

FATSIA and FATSHEDERA
Japanese Aralia

Also called Aralia. This attractive plant with highly glossed leaves makes a handsome indoor pot plant. *Fatsia* may also be grown outdoors in warm, filtered-sun positions, including poolsides, patios, and verandahs.

Grow: In glasshouses and warm bush-houses.
Position indoors: Sunroom or near bright, airy window, indoors.
Water: Keep evenly moist, not over-wet.
Soil: General Potting Mix.
Fertiliser: Complete Plant Food every 2–3 months.
Propagation: From seed.
Pests and problems: Occasionally rotate outdoors.

Varieties include:

FATSIA
F. japonica (Aralia siebondii) (Japan). A compact plant with highly glossed dark-green lobed and pointed leaves. There is also a variegated form *japonica* 'Variegata'.

FATSHEDERA Tree Ivy
F. lizei*. A cross between Fatsia and English Ivy. Five-lobed leaves growing on a fine, wiry, erect stem.
F. lizei variegata*. The green leaves are variegated with creamy white from the margins in.

POLYSCIAS
Aralia

Aralias come from the Pacific Islands. May be grown in greenhouses, and as house plants.

Grow: In warm glasshouses and warm summer bush-houses or outdoors in tropics and subtropics.
Position indoors: Near warm, bright, airy window or in sunroom. Needs sun in winter.

Water: Keep moist, not over-wet.
Soil: General Potting Mix.
Fertiliser: Complete Plant Food in spring, and each month during summer.
Propagation: From cuttings.
Pests and problems: General observation.

Varieties include:
P. balfouriana 'Marginata' (New Caledonia). Variegated Balfour Aralia. Used for hedges in tropics. Grey-green edged in white.
P. fruiticosa (Polynesia, Malaysia, India). Ming Aralia. Dwarf shrub, with narrow, ferny deep green leaves.
P. guilfoylei 'Laciniata'. Resembles 'Victoriae', but larger and more serrated. Grey-green edged white.
P. guilfoylei 'Victoriae' (Polynesia). Lace Aralia. A leafy plant, with grey-green leaves, laced and edged in white.
P. paniculata 'Variegata' (Mauritius). A highly coloured variety, with the leaves variegated between deep green, yellow, cream, and white.

TREVESIA
Snowflake Plant

T. palmata 'Micholitzii' (India) is similar to *Fatsia japonica*, and requires similar growing conditions, although prefers a little more warmth during the growing period.

Position indoors: Prefers greenhouse or sunroom conditions. If indoors it will need to be close to a warm, airy window or glass panel.
Water: Keep moist but not over-wet.
Soil: General Potting Mix.
Fertiliser: Complete Plant Food, monthly.
Propagation: From seed. Cuttings will also strike.
Pests and problems: General observation.

Polyscias balfouriana 'Marginata', Variegated Balfour Aralia

Polyscias fruiticosa, Ming Aralia

Dizygotheca elegantissima, False Aralia

Fatsia japonica 'Variegata', Variegated Japanese Aralia

Fatsia japonica, Japanese Aralia

Trevesia palmata 'Micholitzii', Snowflake Plant

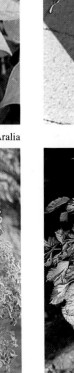

Polyscias guilfoylei 'Laciniata'

Polyscias guilfoylei 'Victoriae', Lace Aralia

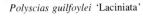

Polyscias paniculata 'Variegata'

ARAUCARIA   Araucariaceae

Norfolk Island Pine

This elegant pine tree is very popular as a potted Christmas tree, for either indoors or patio, or can be planted as a tall outdoor sentinel in the garden.

Grow: As a potted plant, in full sun, in a bush-house or on open verandah, in semi-shade.

Position indoors: Any position receiving good light.

Water: Water thoroughly, but not to excess.

Soil: Indoor Potting Mix.

Fertiliser: Complete Plant Food every 1–2 months, dry, liquid, or foliar.

Propagation: From seeds.

Pests and problems: Watch for scale and mealy bugs. Place out of doors (protected) at first signs of distress.

Varieties include:

A. heterophylla (excelsa) (Norfolk Island). Norfolk Island Pine. Bright-green needles arranged in tiers. When young, widely used as hardy pot plant. Ideal for Christmas decoration.

ARDISIA   Myrsinaceae

Coral Berries

Popular small potted tree with attractive berries, for sheltered outdoors, bush-house, patio, and sunroom.

Grow: In filtered sun to bright light on patio, or in bush-house.

Position indoors: In sunroom or near well-lit window.

Water: Evenly moist.

Soil: General Potting Mix.

Fertiliser: Complete Plant Food (dry, liquid, or foliar) in spring, and then each month.

Propagation: Collect berries and grow seeds.

Pests and problems: Watch for scale insects. Protect from birds to hold berries on plant.

Varieties include:

A. crenata (China). Dark-green glossy foliage; white flowers followed by clusters of red berries in winter.

A. crenata 'Alba'. Identical with the above, but with white berries.

A. crenata 'Variegata'. A new sport, with yellow variegated foliage and red and white variegated berries.

A. humilis (E. Indies). Evergreen shrub, with red tips. Pink flowers are borne continuously, resulting in berries from white to red and finally black.

A. japonica marginata (Japan). Dwarf with deep green leaves edged in white, white flowers and red berries.

Ardisia japonica marginata

Araucaria heterophylla (excelsa), Norfolk Island Pine

Ardisia crenata, Coral Bells

Ardisia crenata 'Variegata'

Ardisia humilis

Ardisia crenata 'Alba'

ASPARAGUS　　　　Liliaceae

Asparagus Fern

Most plant collections would be incomplete without at least one variety of Asparagus Fern. The foliage is valued for its softening appearance, which can be an illusion, as some are quite prickly.

Grow: Adaptable, from open garden groundcover to potted plants in bush-house and on patio.
Position indoors: In airy positions in sunrooms and near well-lit window.
Water: Keep evenly moist, preferably by immersing pots.
Soil: General Potting Mix.
Fertiliser: Complete Plant Food (dry, liquid, or foliar) when repotting and every 2–3 months.
Propagation: From seeds or division.
Pests and problems: Watch for spider mites. Move outdoors at first signs of distress, rotate outdoors.

Varieties include:
A. asparagoides myrtifolius (Cape of Good Hope). Baby Smilax. Twining vine, very dainty, broader leaves than other varieties.
A. densiflorus 'Myers' *(meyerii)* (S. Africa). Showy variety, with stiffly formed fronds of foliage, most attractive.
A. densiflorus 'Sprengeri' (Natal). Widely used indoors, and outside as groundcover. Slightly thorny.
*A. madagascariensis** (Madagascar). Dwarf, warmth-loving variety.
A. retrofactus (S. Africa). Zigzag Shrub, or Tree Asparagus. Small shrub with balls of fine needle-like leaves, new growth bright green.
A. setaceus (plumosus) (S. Africa). Fern Asparagus, with fine foliage on thorny trails.

Asparagus asparagoides myrtifolius, Baby Smilax

Asparagus setaceus (plumosus), Fern Asparagus

Asparagus retrofactus, Tree Asparagus

Asparagus densiflorus 'Sprengeri',
Sprengeri Fern

Asparagus densiflorus 'Myers'
(meyerii), Plume Asparagus

ASPIDISTRA Liliaceae

Cast Iron Plant·

This hardy old-time favourite, remembered from
Grandma's days, is the forerunner of indoor plants.
Grow: Shady areas outside, bush-house, or glasshouse.
Position indoors: Will tolerate poor light, but the better the
position, the better it grows.
Water: Allow to dry before thoroughly watering.
Soil: General Potting Mix.
Fertiliser: Complete Plant Food (liquid or foliar) monthly.
Propagation: By division.
Pests and problems: Few. Watch for scale insects.

Varieties include:
A. elatior* (China). Leathery dark-green foliage.
A. elatior **'Maculata'** (Japan). Milky Way Iron Plant. The dark
green leaves are spotted white.
A. elatior **'Variegata'.** As above, with broad creamy-white
stripe.

Aspidistra elatior 'Maculata', Milky Way Iron Plant

Aspidistra elatior 'Variegata', Variegated Cast Iron Plant

AUCUBA Cornaceae

Gold Dust Plant

These slow-growing, glossy-leafed shrubs are handsome garden specimens for cooler areas. They require filtered sun.

Grow: In semi-shaded gardens, bush-houses, and in pots on cooler, shaded patios, etc.
Position indoors: Airy sunrooms, or for short periods near airy windows.
Water: Allow to dry between waterings.
Soil: General Potting Compost.
Fertiliser: Complete Plant Food (dry, liquid, or foliar) monthly.
Propagation: From cuttings.
Pests and problems: Scale insects. Do not over-water and move outdoors at first sign of distress.

Varieties include:
A. japonica **'Goldiana'*** (Japan). The narrower, serrated leaves are green in the centre, blotched and edged bright yellow to cream.
A. japonica **'Variegata'***. Gold Dust Tree. Stiff, glossy leaves, blotched yellow.
A. japonica **'Crotonifolia'.** Is more vividly variegated.

BEAUCARNEA Liliaceae

Pony Tail

Very adaptable as a garden specimen, or potted feature-plant for indoors or outdoors. Known as Pony Tail, and previously listed as *Noelina*.

Grow: Outdoors, bush-house or open patio, from sun to bright light.
Position indoors: Prefers good light in sunroom or near bright window. Hardy.
Water: Soak well, when dry.
Soil: General Potting Mix.
Fertiliser: Complete Plant Food every 2–3 months (dry, liquid, or foliar).
Propagation: From seeds.
Pests and problems: None observed.

Varieties include:
B. recurvata (Mexico). An unusual small tree, on a swollen trunk, branching with age, with pendulous reed-like leaves. Unusually attractive.

Aucuba japonica 'Crotonifolia', Gold Dust Tree

Beaucarnea recurvata, Pony Tail

BEGONIA   Begoniaceae

Begonias display their beauty in a variety of forms, from the spectacularly colourful foliage of the Rex Begonias, and the magnificent double blooms of the Tuberous Begonias, to the massed colour of the Semperflorens Begonias. All can be displayed to advantage inside or outside the home, in the bush-house or glasshouse, or in the garden.

  While all Begonia varieties are best grown in their own individual outdoor or greenhouse locations, they may also be displayed in the home for varying periods, depending on the position, light, air movement, and care afforded them.

Grow: *Rex Begonias* may be grown in a glasshouse, bush-house, or sheltered patio corner. No sun.
Semperflorens Begonias are very adaptable, tolerating full garden sun to shaded no-sun areas, and flowering most of the year.
Tuberous Begonias are best grown in a glasshouse, or sheltered bush-house as soon as the weather has warmed. Protect dormant tubers during winter. Filtered sun.
  Other Begonia species may be grown in various garden areas, where they should be free from frost and too much sun.
Position indoors: Select an airy, well-lit position with a maximum of filtered sun, for most species. Rex Begonias prefer no sun and are very good subjects in terrariums (an unused fish tank complete with light) where they will brighten up a darker corner for years.
Water: Keep evenly moist during growing season (best immersed), less during dormancy.
Soil: Indoor Potting Mix.
Fertiliser: Complete Plant Food (liquid or foliar) monthly.
Propagation: From seeds, cutting, and division. In the case of Rex Begonias, by leaf segments surrounding a main vein, or even by planting a whole leaf with stem in a sand and peatmoss mixture compost.
Pests and problems: Watch for mildew spots, mainly in autumn and winter.

Varieties include:
B. **'Abel Carriere'.** A showy species with whitish, round leaves and light-green veins; rose-pink flowers.
B. acetosa (Brazil). A rhizomatous variety, which has heart-shaped leaves, green above and maroon beneath, and covered with fine soft hairs, giving the feel and appearance of velvet.
B. sp. × *argentio-guttata** A cane-stem variety, with olive-green leaves, heavily spotted silver, red beneath. Flowers cream with pink.
B. **'Arthur Mallet'*** A beautiful but difficult variety with purplish-red leaves, speckled with silver-pink dots; rose-pink flowers.
B. auriculata (Africa). Cathedral Windows. Fleshy round green leaves marked red and ruffled and twisted; pink flowers.
B. barbana (barkerii). A thick-rhizomed variety, with large light green leaves.
B. **'Beatrice Haddrell'.** Has star-shaped, blackish-brown leaves, with chartreuse markings. Tall spikes of pink flowers.
*B. bowerii** (Chiapas, Mexico). Eyelash Begonia. A small species with numerous small vivid-green leaves and purplish-brown patches and erect hairs along the margins; pink flowers.
B. **'Bow-arriola'.** A rhizomatous cross from Bowerii, with bronzy-green leaves, with purple markings; blush pink flowers.
B. **'Bow-nigra'.** A rhizomatous variety, with star-shaped bronzy leaves with yellowish-green centre-markings and pale-pink flowers.
B. caroliniaefolia (Mexico). A thick rhizomed variety, with palmate leaves, having glossy leaflets on small stalks. Pink flowers.

Begonia acetosa

Begonia epipsala

Begonia barbana (barkerii)

Begonia auriculata, Cathedral Windows

Begonia 'Beatrice Haddrell'

Begonia compta

Begonia 'Bow-arriola'

B. cathayana* (China). Resembling a Rex Begonia with green leaf, broad red veins and silver leaf-blotching; orange flowers.

B. **'Cleopatra'.** Yellow-green maple-leaves with reddish-brown markings towards the margin; pink perfumed flowers.

B. compta (Brazil). A cane-stem variety, tall and slender, with blue-green leaves having silver stripes, and red beneath. White bearded flowers.

B. **'Coral Rubra'.** Cane-stemmed variety, similar to Orange Rubra, but with coral-pink flowers.

B. dayii (Mexico). Attractive rhizome variety, with succulent pale green leaves, having vivid chocolate veins. Ivory flowers.

B. diadema* (Borneo). A fibrous variety, with deeply fingered, brownish-green leaves, with silver markings. Small pink flowers.

B. epipsala (Brazil). Low-growing fibrous variety, with glossy, deep green leaves, which are bright red beneath, covered with brown hairs. White flowers.

Begonia carolinaefolia

Begonia 'Coral Rubra'

Begonia 'Cleopatra'

Begonia 'Abel Carriere'

Begonia 'Bow-nigra'

Begonia dayii

33

BEGONIA, continued

Begonia 'Exotica'

B. sp. × erythrophylla helix. Fleshy green leaves spiralled like a corkscrew; pink flowers.

B. 'Exotica' (New Guinea). A colourful tree variety with green leaves heavily blotched with translucent purple-red.

B. sp. × fuscomaculata. Smooth bronze-green leaves with chocolate spots; pink flowers.

B. sp. × fuchsifoliosa. A vigorous, fleshy, small-leafed variety. Small red flowers.

B. goegoensis (Sumatra). An exotic rhizome variety, the puckered, roundish leaves olive to brown-green, with lighter veins, reddish beneath; pink flowers.

B. sp. × heracleicotyle. Star-shaped, thick, smooth, green leaves are dark edged; pink flowers on long stems.

B. heracleifolia (Mexico). Star Begonia. Has bronzy-green hairy leaves, with green ribs; pink flowers.

Begonia erythrophylla helix

Begonia × fuscomaculata

Begonia goegoensis, Fire-king Begonia

Begonia × heracleicotyle

Begonia × fuchsifoliosa

Begonia heracleifolia, Star Begonia

34

Begonia imperialis, Carpet Begonia

B. hispida cucullifera (Sao Paulo). A fascinating fibrous variety, with soft, hairy, green leaves, from the upper surface of which grow leaflets; white flowers.

B. sp. × *imperiana**. A low-growing variety, appears to be a cathayana-imperialis cross, with soft, furry, deep green leaves, with occasional markings; pinky-orange flowers.

B. imperialis (Mexico). A low-growing, hairy species, with velvety, heart-shaped brownish and green leaves; white flowers. A difficult species.

B. imperialis smaragdina (Mexico). A low plant with emerald-green hairy leaves; white flowers.

B. incana (Mexico). Thick-stemmed, round leaves, covered with white scurf, green only when wet; white flowers.

B. 'Joe Hayden'. The Black Begonia. An upright grower with star-like satiny, bronzy, black-green leaves, red beneath; red winter flowers.

B. kenworthyae (Mexico). Slow-growing, rhizome variety, with ivy-shaped, blue green leaves, having a white centre stripe; pale pink flowers.

Begonia 'Joe Hayden', Black Begonia

Begonia incana

Begonia hispida cucullifera, Piggy-back Begonia

Begonia imperialis smaragdina, Green Carpet Begonia

Begonia kenworthyae

BEGONIA, continued

B. lobata (Brazil). A fibrous variety with glossy deep-green, ivy-shaped leaves, furry brown beneath; white or pink flowers.

B. lubbersii* (Brazil). An exotic upright variety, with narrow, shield-like, bronzy-purple to green leaves, splashed with silver; unusual large single whitish flowers.

B. leptotricha (Paraguay). Wooly Bear. The deep green shiny leaves have brown fur on their undersides, creamy-white flowers, continuously blooming.

B. luxurians (Chile). Tall, with palmate-lobed, fresh-green hairy leaves; cream flowers.

B. 'Mac-Alice'. Resembling Rex Begonia, with rough bluish-green leaves, overlaid faintly with silver and brown; white flowers.

B. manicata 'Aureo-maculata' (Mexico). A robust variety with thick, waxy leaves, resembling a Rex Begonia, with yellow blotches; tiny pink flowers.

B. manicata 'Crispa'. A slow-growing variety with large, fleshy, waxy, light-green leaves, their margins wavy and deeply crested.

Begonia manicata 'Crispa'

Begonia lobata

Begonia luxurians, Palm Leaf Begonia

Begonia manicata 'Aureo-maculata', Leopard Begonia

Begonia leptotricha, Woolly Bear

Begonia 'Mac-Alice'

Begonia mazae 'Stitchleaf', Stitchleaf Begonia

Begonia metallica, Metallic Leaf Begonia

B. masoniana (Malaya). Iron Cross. A much-prized species with hairy, puckered, nile-green leaves, nicely marked with a bold reddish-brown 'cross' pattern; greenish-white flowers, with red bristles.

B. mazae (Chiapas, Mexico). A rhizomatous variety, with fleshy roundish leaves, light green to bronzy, with purple markings; pink flowers.

B. mazae nigricans* (Chiapas, Mexico). A small variety with roundish, satiny bronze-green leaves, with a bronzy-black pattern; pink flowers.

***B. mazae* 'Stitchleaf'.** Similar to the above, with light-green leaves and purple markings, resembling stitches along the edge of the leaf.

B. metallica (Bahia). A bushy, fibrous-rooted variety with metallic-green leaves, depressed purplish veins which also show beneath; showy pink flowers.

B. olbia (Brazil). A small fibrous variety, with bronzy thin leaves, dark veins, and greenish white flowers.

B. olsoniae (Vellozoana) (Brazil). A beautiful rhizome variety, the green and brownish-green leaves having contrasting ivory veins; whitish flowers.

Begonia masoniana, Iron Cross Begonia

Begonia olsoniae (vellozoana)

Begonia mazae

Begonia olbia

BEGONIA, continued

B. **'Orange Rubra'.** A beautiful tree begonia with silver-spotted leaves, and striking clusters of clear orange waxy flowers.

B. paulensis (Brazil). A beautiful rhizome variety, with large, rounded, fresh green leaves, heavily corrugated and prominent veins. Red bearded flowers.

B. sp. × *pearlii* (Pearlite). Resembling a Rex, with green to bronzy-green leaves, pebbled all over with a pearly sheen; white flowers.

B. **'Perle Lorraine'.** A slender, bushy, fibrous variety with the green leaves netted with chocolate markings; pink flowers in winter.

B. purity. A low grower, with fresh green (occasionally bronzy-green) leaves; pure white flowers.

B. pustulata argentea (Mexico). A beautiful low-growing variety with plush nile-green leaves, richly variegated with silver and brown; greenish flowers.

B. rex. (See separate section).

Begonia 'Orange Rubra'

Begonia 'Perle Lorraine'

Begonia pustulata argentea

Begonia paulensis

Begonia purity

Begonia × *pearlii*

B. **'Ricky Minter'.** A rhizomatous variety with bronzy frilled leaves; pink flowers.

B. **'Rogerii'***. A fibrous variety, with glossy, olive-green leaves, browning from the veins. Pink flowers, similar to Scharffii.

B. **rubro-venia 'Silver'*** (Bhutan). An upright grower with narrow metallic silver leaves, which are red beneath; white flowers, veined red.

B. **sceptrum** (Brazil). A fibrous-rooted variety with deeply fingered green leaves, spotted silver; pink flowers.

B. **scharffii** (Brazil). Elephant's Ear Begonia. Similar to the above, with deep green white-hairy leaves, red beneath; showy pink flowers.

B. **schmidtiana** (Brazil). A low-growing, fibrous variety with olive-green hairy leaves, reddish beneath; small pink flowers.

B. **semperflorens** (Brazil). Wax Begonias. See separate section.

B. **serratipetala*** (New Guinea). Gold Medal. An upright-growing species with glossy, narrow, reddish leaves spotted red to pink; flowers deep pink.

B. **'Silver Pearl'.*** Of Rex habit, with leaves of glistening silver pearl spots, shining through a grey-brown leaf.

B. **'Silver Star'.** A rhizomatous variety with star-shaped green leaves overlaid with silver; white flowers.

B. **tuberous.** See separate section.

B. **vitifolia** (Brazil). An upright growing variety, very similar to Lobata, but thicker stemmed and more compact growth. Good heads of white flowers.

Begonia schmidtiana

Begonia vitifolia

Begonia 'Ricky Minter'

Begonia 'Silver Star'

Begonia scharffii, Elephant's Ear Begonia

Begonia sceptrum

BEGONIA, continued

REX BEGONIAS

Among the showiest of foliage plants, mostly bearing waxy flowers during late summer and autumn. (Assam.)

Varieties include:

***B. rex* 'American Beauty'.** A medium-sized glossy leaf, silver at first, then turning metallic deep red, with black centre and edge.

***B. rex* 'Armada'.** The centre is bronze-green, zoned with bright-green and white spots, and edged with bronze-red.

***B. rex* 'Beauty'.** A colourful free-growing variety, with silver leaves flushed pink, black centre veins, and black and green edge markings.

***B. rex* 'Bella'.** Sharkskin. Silver-grey leaf overlaid with mauve, edging and centre-markings blackish purple. Texture of leaf resembles that of sharkskin.

***B. rex* 'Black Prince'.** Deep brownish-green leaf with silver bubble-markings.

***B. rex* 'Bright Christmas'.** A contrasting vivid leaf with black centre, and a broad zone of silver flushed red, and margin of vivid green with red edging.

Begonia rex 'American Beauty'

Begonia rex 'Beauty'

Begonia rex 'Bella'

Begonia rex 'Armada'

Begonia rex 'Black Prince'

40   *Begonia rex* 'Bright Christmas'

B. rex 'Bright Dawn'. A small grey leaf heavily spotted black with a purple overlay and numerous purple hairs.

B. rex 'Bright Star'. A star-shaped leaf in black and silver.

B. rex 'Brilliance'. A vivid leaf of bubbly silver, with deep green along the veins, and vivid red centre and edging.

B. rex 'Bronze King'. Heavily fluted and spiralled leaf of bronze-green to deep red, with silver spots, and red hairy stems.

B. rex 'Brown Satin'. Brownish scaly leaves banded in fresh green; juvenile leaves are black, banded in green.

B. rex 'Can Can'. A larger edition of Pink Beauty. A heavily serrated leaf of silver, overlaid and edged in pink and red.

Begonia rex 'Bright Star'

Begonia rex 'Brilliance'

Begonia rex 'Bronze King'

Begonia rex 'Bright Dawn'

Begonia rex 'Brown Satin'

Begonia rex 'Can Can'

41

BEGONIA, continued

B. rex **'Carmelita'.** Low-growing, heavily spiralled leaf, bright green, with bronze centre and margin, and silver blotches and spots overlaid pink.

B. rex **'Christmas'.** Roundish silver leaf, with dark centre and veins, green outer band with red edging, bright pink overlay.

B. rex **'Christmas Twist'.** Spiralled and serrated leaf of deep green, with red leaf margin and silver blotches and spots, overlaid with pink.

B. rex **'Cordoza Gardens'.** Large leaves with centre blackish-red, surrounded by silver and emerald green, with a red leaf-margin.

B. rex **'Crimson Glow'.** Small leaf, with centre of bronze-red shading to silvery-green and edged in bronze-red.

B. rex **'Crimson Satin'.** A dwarf small leaf of unusual colouring, with a black centre zone, then a zone of silver, and black margin. The entire leaf is covered with a crimson to purple overlay.

Begonia rex 'Christmas'

Begonia rex 'Carmelita'

Begonia rex 'Christmas Twist'

Begonia rex 'Cordoza Gardens'

Begonia rex 'Crimson Glow'

Begonia rex 'Crimson Satin'

Begonia rex 'Curly Impression'

B. rex 'Curly Fireflush'. A corkscrew variety with fresh-green leaves edged and centre-marked red; the leaf is covered in soft red hairs, which glisten in certain lights, resembling red velvet.

B. rex 'Curly Impression'. The lightly spiralled blackish leaves, banded silver, become heavily flushed with reddish-purple.

B. rex 'Curly Merry Christmas'. A corkscrew variety, resembling Merry Christmas, but lacking a little of that rich colouring.

B. rex 'Curly Metallica'. The lightly spiralled, glossy, silver-marked green leaves become flushed with metallic red.

B. rex 'Dark Cloud'. Smallish leaf, slightly hairy and silvery; edging and centre markings deep blackish-green.

B. rex 'Dark Night'. An attractive variety; the centre margin is black, surrounded by blackish green, then a shining silver margin, then bright green, with a blackish outer margin.

B. rex 'Dawn'. Flat greenish-grey leaves flushed pink and silver bubble-markings.

Begonia rex 'Curly Merry Christmas'

Begonia rex 'Curly Metallica'

Begonia rex 'Dark Cloud'

Begonia rex 'Curly Fireflush'

Begonia rex 'Dark Night'

Begonia rex 'Dawn'

43

BEGONIA, continued

B. rex 'Dew Drop'. A miniature variety, with rounded, very small, silver-grey glossy leaves.

B. rex 'Don'. A nicely spiralled leaf of silver, overlaid with pink, and an outer zone of greenish black.

B. rex 'Double Impression'. Silver-grey leaf, later turning rosy-purple, edged and centre-marked blackish purple.

B. rex 'Dusk'. Dark greenish-brown centre and spotting along the veins and margin, remainder of leaf silver.

B. rex 'Dusky Rose'. Has silvery veins, bordered in blackish-green, and the remainder of the leaf spotted silver, suffused with metallic red.

B. rex 'Edna Korts'. Spiralled leaf with bronze centre, silver margin, and green outer margin with red edging, pink overlay.

Begonia rex 'Dew Drop'

Begonia rex 'Dusky Rose'

Begonia rex 'Don'

Begonia rex 'Edna Korts'

Begonia rex 'Double Impression'

Begonia rex 'Dusk'

44

B. rex 'Emerald Beauty'. Medium-sized silver leaf surrounded and centre-margined with emerald green.

B. rex 'Emerald Giant'. Formerly Green Perfection. A striking variety, with the centre of the leaf blackish-green, banded silver-grey and margined vivid emerald-green, with red edging.

B. rex 'Evergreen'. Smallish leaf of silver and bright green, with a bronze edging.

B. rex 'Exotic'. Smallish brown-green leaves splashed with silver blotches between the veins.

B. rex 'Fairy'. Of strong habit with the silver puckered leaves veined and margined in brownish-green.

B. rex 'Fairy' (Melbourne strain). Silver leaf, with indented veins of bronze-green, and pink overlay.

Begonia rex 'Exotic'

Begonia rex 'Evergreen'

Begonia rex 'Emerald Giant'

Begonia rex 'Emerald Beauty'

Begonia rex 'Fairy'

Begonia rex 'Fairy' (Melbourne strain)

45

BEGONIA, continued

B. rex 'Fantasy'. A smooth, flattish leaf, silver between the veins, with a metallic-purple sheen, the margin and centre brownish-green.

B. rex 'Fiesta'. A small variety with soft hairy leaves of green, later pinkish-brown spotted and blotched silver.

B. rex 'Filligree'. A sharply lobed leaf of silver, with deep green along the veins and margin, and pink blister patches.

B. rex 'Forest Lake'*. A slightly spiralled leaf, mostly silver, with an outer zone of bright green.

B. rex 'Frau Hoffman'. The juvenile leaf is silvery white, with the centre and edging blackish-red, later spreading until the leaf is blackish-red.

B. rex 'Glory of St. Albans'. Bright rosy-purple small-leafed variety, edged and centre-veined with blackish-purple.

B. rex 'Glory Princess'. A smallish spiralled leaf of silver, heavily spotted on edges with black, purplish pink centre and margin flush.

Begonia rex 'Glory of St Albans'

Begonia rex 'Frau Hoffman'

Begonia rex 'Filligree'

Begonia rex 'Fiesta'

Begonia rex 'Glory Princess'

Begonia rex 'Fantasy'

B. rex **'Gorgeous'***. Well described, an extremely glossy silver corkscrewed leaf, edged bronzy red.

B. rex **'Greenberry'**. The sturdy leaves are marked in varying shades of green—deep, emerald, and pale—intermingled with silver dots; red edging.

B. rex **'Green Countess'**. A corkscrew variety with the bright-green soft leaves speckled with silver dots.

B. rex **'Green Ripple.'** A smooth-edged leaf of silver-green, with a reddish leaf margin.

B. rex **'Green Velvet'***. A deep green leaf with silver blotches between the veins.

B. rex **'Grey Ghost'**. The silver leaf has brownish veins and is flushed on the edges with metallic rosy-purple.

B. rex **'Grey Maraka'**. A rather hairy silver-grey leaf with dark coloured veins.

B. rex **'Helen Teupel'**. Long-fringed leaves with edging and veins of metallic green and leaf-bubbles of bright rosy-purple.

Begonia rex 'Grey Ghost'

Begonia rex 'Helen Teupel'

Begonia rex 'Grey Maraka'

Begonia rex 'Greenberry'

Begonia rex 'Green Countess'

Begonia rex 'Green Ripple'

47

BEGONIA, continued

B. rex 'Helen Tuppel'. A true Rex, differing from Helen Teupel. Has deeply toothed leaves of blackish-bronze, with silver blotches, which turn reddish-purple.

B. rex 'Her Majesty'. A broad leaf, reddish-purple with a green zone, speckled with silver dots.

B. rex 'His Majesty'. Long, pointed and notched, blackish-maroon leaves, with a broad silver zone, overlaid with purple.

B. rex 'Hottentot'. A corkscrew variety with silver-green leaf veined with deep green and edged with pink; leaf covered with whitish hairs.

B. rex 'Irish Colleen'. The satiny vivid emerald-green leaves are veined and margined in black.

B. rex 'Kathleyana'. Deep-green leaves, heavily speckled with silver except at the veins and centre of the leaf.

Begonia rex 'Her Majesty'

Begonia rex 'Hottentot'

Begonia rex 'His Majesty'

Begonia rex 'Irish Colleen'

Begonia rex 'Helen Tuppel'

Begonia rex 'Kathleyana'

48

B. rex 'King Henry VII'. Deep maroon, deeper in centre, surrounded by silver-grey and edged with maroon.
B. rex 'King Henry' sport. Similar to King Henry, but with a bright pink overlay, instead of crimson.
B. rex 'La Marque'. A nicely spiralled white leaf, with fine olive-green veins and red leaf margin.
B. rex 'Lillian'. A beautifully spiralled leaf of smooth silver, with an outer margin of bright green spotted silver, red edging. There is another strain of Lillian in the Melbourne area.
B. rex 'Lorraine Closson'. A dwarf variety, also called Cardinal, with dark metallic red leaves, marked black.

Begonia rex 'La Marque'

Begonia rex **'King Henry' sport**

Begonia rex 'Lillian'

Begonia rex 'Lorraine Closson'

Begonia rex 'Lillian' (Melbourne strain)

Begonia rex 'King Henry VII'

49

BEGONIA, continued

B. rex 'Merry Christmas'. Beautifully defined leaf, centre velvety red, surrounded by broad silver zone, suffused pink—outer zone fresh green, edged red.

B. rex 'Louise Closson'. (Ajax) Brilliantly coloured leaf of crimson, with black centre and green margin with black edging.

B. rex 'Lucilie Closson'. Smallish leaf of green and silver, later black and silver, with a purplish-red overlay.

B. rex 'Lucy Closson'. (Patsy) A dark, almost black leaf, showing blotches of purple and silver.

B. rex 'Majestic'. A silver-grey leaf, with the centre and margin zone blue-green, with silver-grey speckles showing through; outer margin reddish.

B. rex 'Marion Louise'. A sharply lobed silver leaf, distinctly marked with the centre veins and margin blackish, surrounded by green.

B. rex 'Mauve Gem'*. A handsome spiralled leaf of silver, overlaid with mauve, and an outer zone of blackish-purple, speckled with silver.

Begonia rex 'Lucille Closson'

Begonia rex 'Louise Closson'

Begonia rex 'Majestic'

Begonia rex 'Lucy Closson'

Begonia rex 'Merry Christmas'

50   *Begonia rex* 'Marion Louise'

Begonia rex 'Metallica'

B. rex 'Metallica'. A beautiful species with silver-grey leaf, edged and centre-veined with green, the silver-grey later turning metallic red.

B. rex 'Meteor'. Background of rose, speckled over with greenish-silver.

B. rex 'Midnight'. The quilted leaves are deep burgundy-red, without marking.

B. rex 'Mikado'. Centre of leaf blackish-purple, surrounded by silver-grey, suffused with pink, and edged with purple.

B. rex 'Mountain Stream'. An iridescent silver leaf, zoned with green blotches, and edged in reddish-purple; centre has black veins and is suffused with pink.

B. rex 'Mr Wren'. Bluish-green to bronze-green leaf, covered with white hairs and fine, silver spots.

Begonia rex 'Mountain Stream'

Begonia rex 'Midnight'

Begonia rex 'Mr Wren'

Begonia rex 'Meteor'

Begonia rex 'Mikado'

51

BEGONIA, continued

B. rex 'Mystic'. Silver leaf, with black centre and edge, pink overlay, later red.

B. rex 'Mystic Twist'. A spiralled silver leaf, with blackish centre and leaf margin, pink overlay.

B. rex 'Octopus'. A nicely spiralled green leaf, heavily spotted with silver, deep red margin.

B. rex 'Ojai'. A spiralled leaf of silver, with green and silver zone edged red, blackish centre.

B. rex 'Paree'. A thickish leaf, entirely silver, covered by red hairs, and with green centre veins and margin markings.

B. rex 'Peace'. Silver leaves with a blackish-green star centre-marking, pink flushing from the centre and edge.

Begonia rex 'Mystic'

Begonia rex 'Peace'

Begonia rex 'Paree'

Begonia rex 'Ojai'

Begonia rex 'Mystic Twist'

Begonia rex 'Octopus'

B. rex 'Pearl Ripple'. Large blackish-green leaf, with round pearl-white raised blotches; some leaves are suffused with pinkish-purple.

B. rex 'Perle Eclipse'*. The spiralled silver-white leaf has bronze-green vein markings.

B. rex 'Pink Beauty'. An American variety with small cupped leaves of silver-grey, edged and suffused with pink at veins.

B. rex 'Pink Pearl'. The leaf entirely consists of silver-pink bubbles, with a red leaf margin, and sunken veins of pale green.

B. rex 'President Carnot'. Blackish-green leaf, with large areas and bubbles of silver-grey.

B. rex 'Princess'. A pretty variety with the silver leaf having red centre veins and leaf margin, and a fresh-green zone towards the margin; the silver is overlaid with metallic pink near the centre.

B. rex 'Prince Charming'. Roundish leaf of silver, flushed pink, with deep green centre and edge markings, forming a silver star.

Begonia rex 'President Carnot'

Begonia rex 'Pink Pearl'

Begonia rex 'Princess'

Begonia rex 'Prince Charming'

Begonia rex 'Pearl Ripple'

Begonia rex 'Pink Beauty'

53

BEGONIA, continued

B. rex 'Purple Curly Stardust'. A beautiful spiralled variety, juvenile green, later purple completely spotted with silver.

B. rex 'Purple Haze'. Brownish-purple leaf, with fine spotting and occasional blotches of silver.

B. rex 'Queen Wilhelmina'*. A slightly quilted leaf, silver-white with a few faint bronze green markings.

B. rex 'Radiant'. A blackish-green leaf, with deep red centre and margin, and numerous silver and pink spots.

B. rex 'Red Ripple'. Brilliantly coloured, metallic red on blackish green.

B. rex 'Red Robin'. A highly coloured miniature variety; the small silver-grey leaves with blackish markings become flushed all over with deep metallic-red; a slow grower.

B. rex 'Rosella'. Reddish brown with a broad centre zone of bright green.

Begonia rex 'Red Ripple'

Begonia rex 'Radiant'

Begonia rex 'Purple Curly Stardust'

Begonia rex 'Purple Haze'

Begonia rex 'Red Robin'

Begonia rex 'Rosella'

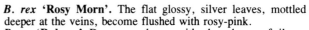

B. rex **'Rosy Morn'**. The flat glossy, silver leaves, mottled deeper at the veins, become flushed with rosy-pink.
B. rex **'Rubena'**. Deep-green leaves with a broad zone of silver.
B. rex **'Salamander'**. Deeply fingered leaves of rich forest-green with bubble areas of silver.
B. rex **'Sampson'**. A strong growing variety, with bold, slightly hairy leaves with zones of brownish-green and silver.
B. rex **'Salt 'n' Pepper'**. Blackish-green, heavily spotted silver, slightly spiralled.
B. rex **'San Mateo'**. Corkscrew variety, forest-green, with large spotted areas of silver, and purple-pink.

Begonia rex 'Salt 'n' Pepper'

Begonia rex 'Rubena'

Begonia rex 'Rosy Morn'

Begonia rex 'San Mateo'

Begonia rex 'Salamander'

Begonia rex 'Sampson'

55

BEGONIA, continued

B. rex 'Shot Silk'. An attractive corkscrew leaf of silver, very finely spotted red-bronze in zones, and shot with tones of red, pink, purple, and green.

B. rex 'Shower of Stars'. Dark blackish-green leaf, heavily spotted with silver between the veins.

B. rex 'Silver Curl'. A vigorous spiralled variety, with silver-grey leaves, finely spotted with dark grey around the veins and leaf margins.

B. rex 'Silver Circle'. A deep green leaf, later brownish, with a contrasting circular leaf zone of silver.

B. rex 'Silver Corkscrew'. A beautifully spiralled leaf of vivid green and pure silver.

B. rex 'Silver Dawn'*. Blackish-grey leaves mottled with silver.

B. rex 'Silver Dove'. Silver-grey leaf with a pinkish sheen; red margin and centre-veining, on underside of leaf, shows through.

Begonia rex 'Silver Circle'

Begonia rex 'Shower of Stars'

Begonia rex 'Silver Curl'

Begonia rex 'Silver Dove'

Begonia rex 'Silver Corkscrew'

56

Begonia rex 'Shot Silk'

B. rex **'Silver Dust'.** Small dark bronze leaf, finely spotted silver, occasional pink overlay.

B. rex **'Silver Filligree'.** The all-silver leaves have bright to deep green veining.

B. rex **'Silver Glow'***. A bold corkscrew leaf of silver-white, heavily veined deep green.

B. rex **'Silver Greenheart'.** Small puckered leaf of silver, deep green veins and striped margin zone.

B. rex **'Silverheart'.** A spiralled leaf, at first appearance resembling a heart, of silver flushed pink, with blackish-red margin and centre, and an outer band of green.

B. rex **'Silver Lake'***. A nicely spiralled silver leaf, speckled black along the veins and margin.

B. rex **'Silver Mist'.** (Grey Ghost) A silver leaf, with black centre, and purple edging flushing inwards.

B. rex **'Silver Queen'.** Silver-grey leaf with centre-veining and edging of deep green.

Begonia rex 'Silver Filigree'

Begonia rex 'Silver Greenheart'

Begonia rex 'Silver Mist'

Begonia rex 'Silver Queen'

Begonia rex 'Silver Dust'

Begonia rex 'Silverheart'

BEGONIA, continued

B. rex 'Silver Speckle'. Medium-sized, bright-green leaves heavily speckled with silver dots on the raised areas between the veins.

B. rex 'Silver Sweet'. Glistening silver leaf with black margin and centre-markings.

B. rex 'Silver Twist'. A spiralled variety, with olive to brown-green leaves, with a margin and spotting of silver-white.

B. rex 'Sir Percy'. A smallish leaf of silver, edged and backed, in deep red.

B. rex 'Solid Silver'. Broad, roundish leaves, entirely silver.

B. rex 'Souvenier'. Medium-sized, crimple-edged, fawn-silver leaves veined and margin-spotted red.

Begonia rex 'Silver Speckle'

Begonia rex 'Silver Twist'

Begonia rex 'Sir Percy'

Begonia rex 'Silver Sweet'

Begonia rex 'Solid Silver'

Begonia rex 'Souvenier'

B. rex 'Spider'. Small grey-to-white serrated leaf, with black spider-in-web-like markings.

B. rex 'Strawberry Sundae'*. A slightly spiralled leaf of silver, overlaid red and green, and deep red veins.

B. rex 'Summer Fair'. (New American) Beautiful bright-green leaves colourfully marked with pink and silver.

B. rex 'Summer Maid'. Similar to the above in colouring, but the leaves are smaller, and the markings slightly different.

B. rex 'Sunburst'. Heavily serrated corkscrew leaf of bronze-green, with silver blotches and spotting, overlaid pink and red.

B. rex 'Storm Cloud'. Silver-grey leaves with black veins, surrounded by deep-grey stippling and pinkish-grey leaf-edging.

B. rex 'Teardrop'. A tear shaped small silver leaf, with black margin and centre vein markings, and with a bright pink to red overlay.

Begonia rex 'Spider'

Begonia rex 'Summer Fair'

Begonia rex 'Summer Maid'

Begonia rex 'Storm Cloud'

Begonia rex 'Teardrop'

Begonia rex 'Sunburst'

BEGONIA, continued

B. rex 'The Kaiser'. Deep-green leaf, spotted silver and with blackish-red edging.

B. rex 'Tinsel'. A silver leaf with tinsel-red flush, and blackish-purple veins and margin.

B. rex 'Vesuvius'. Iridescent blackish-red leaf, with silver to red leaf spots.

B. rex 'Westland Beauty'. A silver leaf flushed pink, with brown centre and veins, and bronze-green margin.

B. rex 'Westland Pride'. Silver leaf, with dark veins, and dark centre and margin spotting, purple centre and margin overlay.

B. rex 'Winter Queen'. A heavily serrated and ruffled corkscrew of silver, with deep olive-green markings.

B. rex 'Yuletide'. A brilliant Merry Christmas cross with large silver spots.

Begonia rex 'Westland Beauty'

Begonia rex 'Tinsel'

Begonia rex 'The Kaiser'   *Begonia rex* 'Westland Pride'

Begonia rex 'Yuletide'

Begonia rex 'Vesuvius'

60   *Begonia rex* 'Winter Queen'

SEMPERFLORENS BEGONIAS

Wax or Bedding Begonias, with waxy leaves, and single or double flowers, dwarf in growth and ideal for semi-shaded positions. (Brazil.)

Varieties include:

B. semperflorens **'albo-foliis'.** Calla Lily Begonia. A dwarf Wax Begonia; glossy-green leaves splashed and mottled with white; pink flowers.

B. s. fl. pl. **'Ballet'.** Small and compact bronze-leafed variety, with numerous double white flowers.

B.s. **'Charm'.** Free growing, with the green leaves freely splashed cream, single pink flowers.

B.s. fl. pl. **'Dolly Varden'*.** A dwarf variety; pale-green leaves edged red; small double, pale-pink flowers.

B.s. fl. pl. **'Firefly'*.** A dwarf variety with dark coppery foliage; double red flowers, with crested yellow centre. Similar to 'Robin Hood', only red.

B.s. fl. pl. **'Goldilocks'.** A bronze-leafed variety, with double deep pink flowers, with orange crested centres.

B.s. fl. pl. **'Jewelite'.** A bronze-leafed variety, with deep pink, lightly packed, multi-centred, double flowers.

B.s. fl. pl. **'Pink Camellia'.** A dwarf, bushy variety with highly-glossed deep-red leaves; clusters of double pink, small, camellia-like flowers in profusion.

Begonia semperflorens albo-foliis, Calla Lily Begonia

Begonia semperflorens 'Charm'

Begonia semperflorens fl. pl. 'Goldilocks'

Begonia semperflorens fl. pl. 'Ballet'

Begonia semperflorens fl. pl. 'Jewelite'

Begonia semperflorens fl. pl. 'Pink Camellia'

61

BEGONIA, continued

B.s. fl. pl. **'Pink Poi'.** Has green foliage, and medium sized pom-pom pink flowers.

B.s. **'Prince Charming'.** The outer petals are large and broad, centre tufted pink and yellow, on green foliage.

B.s. fl. pl. **'Red Camellia'*.** Similar to 'Pink Camellia' but with red camellia-shaped flowers.

B.s. fl. pl. **'Red Poi'.** A strong grower, with green foliage, and large (up to 5 cm) red pom-pom flowers.

B.s. fl. pl. **'Robin Hood'.** Bronzy foliage with pale-pink flowers with crested yellow centres.

B.s. fl. pl. **'Rosy O'Grady'.** Masses of small double rosy-red flowers, on green foliage.

Begonia semperflorens 'Prince Charming'

Begonia semperflorens fl. pl. 'Pink Poi'

Begonia semperflorens fl. pl. 'Red Poi'

Begonia semperflorens fl. pl. 'Rosy O'Grady'

Begonia semperflorens fl. pl. 'Robin Hood'

B.s. 'Thousand Wonders'. F.1. hybrid, dwarf variety for borders, producing thousands of flowers over a long period. Colours of red, pink, and white, from seed.

B.s. fl. pl. 'Tinkerbell'. A deep pink sort of Firefly, with the same shaped flowers and bronze foliage.

B.s. fl. pl. 'Variegata'. Bronzy foliage with double camellia-shaped bright-pink flowers, variegated deep pink.

B.s. fl. pl. 'White Poi'. Has green foliage and multi-centred balls of white flowers, tinged mauve.

B.s. fl. pl. 'White Christmas'*. A dwarf variety; waxy green leaves; a profusion of double white flowers.

Begonia semperflorens fl. pl. 'Tinkerbell'

Begonia semperflorens fl. pl. 'Variegata'

Begonia semperflorens 'Thousand Wonders', Red

Begonia semperflorens 'Thousand Wonders', White

Begonia semperflorens fl. pl. 'White Poi'

Begonia semperflorens 'Thousand Wonders', Pink

63

BEGONIA, continued

TUBEROUS BEGONIAS (Tuberhybrida)

A bulbous variety, summer growing and winter dormant, with watery stems and brittle, light-green, pointed leaves. Beautiful single or double flowers of different type and colours; a feature of many of our parks.
Varieties include:
B.t. **'Camellia'.** Large double flowers of formal shape, tuberous in self colours.
B.t. **'Fimbriata'** (Fringed or Ruffled). Similar to the above but with petals serrated and frilled at the edges.
B.t. **'Picottee'.** Similar to 'Camellia', but with two-tone colour combinations, in many shades.
B.t. ***pendula*** (Hanging Basket Begonias). Numerous single, to fully double flowers, a little smaller than the above varieties, on pendulous stems.

Begonia tuberhybrida 'Fimbriata', Apricot Pink

Begonia tuberhybrida 'Camellia', Red

Begonia tuberhybrida 'Camellia', colour selection

Begonia tuberhybrida 'Picottee'

Begonia tuberhybrida 'Fimbriata', Apricot

Begonia tuberhybrida 'Fimbriata', Re

Begonia tuberhybrida pendula, colour selection

64

BRASSAIA and SCHEFFLERA

Araliaceae

Umbrella Trees

Excellent and hardy potted trees. One of the most widely used commercial indoor plants. Attractive glossy foliage.

Grow: Outdoors, as garden tree, or in pots on patios, around pools, and in bush-houses.

Position indoors: From full sun to good light, very hardy; best multiple-planted.

Water: Thoroughly wet and allow to dry between waterings.

Soil: General Potting Mix.

Fertiliser: Complete Plant Food (liquid or foliar) monthly.

Propagation: From seeds, or sometimes by cuttings.

Pests and problems: Few. Occasionally aphis, scale insects, or caterpillars.

Varieties include:

BRASSAIA

B. actinophylla (Queensland, New Guinea, Java). Queensland Umbrella Tree. Glossy green foliage, rapid growth, tall growing tree with red flower spikes.

B. actinophylla **'Variegata'**. An interesting variegated form.

SCHEFFLERA

S. arboricola (Taiwan). Fast-growing, branching plant of dwarf habit, with glossy green palmate leaves. Clustered flowers.

S. digitata (New Zealand). Somewhat resembling the above, but the palmate leaves are more pointed, with wavy edges.

Schefflera digitata, New Zealand Seven Fingers

Brassaia actinophylla, Queensland Umbrella Tree

Schefflera arboricola, Dwarf Umbrella Tree

Brassaia actinophylla – with flower spike

Brassaia actinophylla 'Variegata', Variegated Umbrella Tree

65

BROMELIADS   Bromeliaceae

Bromeliads are members of the Pineapple family. In their natural environments of Brazil and other South American countries they may be found growing high up in trees, or among rocks, or even as ground plants on the jungle floor. Some have rather insignificant greenish rosettes of leaves, but are capable of producing the most beautiful and highly coloured flower-spikes, some short-lived, others lasting for many months. Other varieties have attractive cross-banding, or unusual leaf-markings, while others again may be variegated or flushed with pink, red, or other colourings.

Bromeliads are very easily grown because they will tolerate a wide range of growing conditions from near-freezing to tropical jungles. They will usually stand for long periods as indoor plants with a minimum of attention, requiring only their centre well to be kept full of water, and a small amount of sunshine or good light. They are best grown in ferneries, under the shelter of trees, on protected patios, on airy verandas, or in glasshouses. They may be grown in smallish pots, hanging baskets, slabs of tree fern, or in open garden beds. They prefer a very well drained potting medium, such as shredded tree fern, orchid compost, or a similarly made-up mixture of peatmoss, leaf mould, coarse sand, and charcoal; I have even grown them in coarse river sand alone. Occasional feeding or wetting-down of the foliage with a mild liquid fertiliser, perhaps monthly, is also beneficial in maintaining a healthy appearance.

Flowering:
Bromeliads flower at different periods of the year, and will do so when the plants have matured sufficiently. Some varieties such as Billbergia have beautiful flowers which only last one week, whereas others, like Aechmeas and Vrieseas, may remain attractive for up to 5 months.

Premature flowering of mature plants may be induced in a number of ways, the most common one being to supply the plant with ethylene gas. A simple way of doing this is to drain off the water and place the plant, pot and all, in a large plastic bag with a ripe apple (these give off ethylene gas). The bag should be tied and placed for about 10 days in light, but not sun. The plant is then removed and a flower spike should appear within one or two months.

Another method is to pour a solution containing 7 gm of calcium carbide in 1 litre of water, into the emptied water well of the Bromeliad. Other products now used by commercial pineapple growers are also available.

Propagation:
Bromeliads reproduce either from seed, by division, or by suckers. For commercial growing, seeds may be obtained, and should be planted immediately, as they are very short-lived. From seeds, most Bromeliads reach flowering size in 4–7 years. Many varieties produce suckers following maturity or flowering of the plant. However, one should not be tempted to remove these prematurely, but should wait until they become strong enough. Remember also to leave one or two suckers attached to the parent plant, as this eventually dies after flowering, and if all the suckers have been removed, the variety could then be lost. Larger and older clumps of Bromeliads can be divided up at any time. Sucker plants usually flower in 1–2 years.

Varieties:
These days there are over 2,000 species of Bromeliads, from the fruiting Pineapple, to the spectacular Vrieseas, and the hanging Spanish Moss of the Florida swamps. Almost daily there are new varieties being hybridised. The following is a listing of many popular ones being used as house plants.

ACANTHOSTACHYS
Pine-cone Bromeliad

This unusual, stiff, stringy bromeliad clusters freely, and is adaptable as a house plant. It is best grown in a hanging basket or pot, which suits its cascading habit.
Light: Moderate to bright light.
Water: Keep moist but not over-wet.
Soil: Orchid Compost.
Fertiliser: Liquid fertiliser to the soil, monthly.
Comments: Adaptable for hanging pots or baskets.
Propagation: By division.

Varieties include:
*A. strobilacea** (S. Brazil). Narrow leaves, inflorescence of red cone-like fruit.

AECHMEA

Quite hardy indoors. The large and colourful flower spikes are long-lasting. Many varieties have colourful foliage and the flower spike is an added bonus to an already attractive plant.

Light: Bright light to filtered sun.
Water: Keep water in well at all times. Allow soil of stiffer varieties to dry between waterings. Mist foliage regularly.
Soil: Orchid Compost with added peatmoss.
Fertiliser: Liquid fertiliser to the soil, monthly.
Comments: Once a matured plant has flowered it will eventually die. However it usually suckers new plants, which will probably flower the following year.
Propagation: By separating and growing large off-shoots.

Varieties include:
A. angustifolia (northern S. America). Showy yellow-green leaves of medium size, flushed reddish-brown, and blue and white berries, after yellow flowers.
A. 'Bert'. Matte-green leaves with purple-brown crossbands and heavy dark spines. Arching inflorescence with red bract.
A. bracteata (Central America). A sturdy, bright green rosette, with large spines. The inflorescence of bright red bracts with greenish-yellow petals, followed by black berries.
A. caudata (Brazil). Medium green leaves and inflorescence of golden yellow bract on a white stem.
A. caudata variegata (Brazil). A sparsely leafed variety, with stiff green leaves, banded cream; attractive red bract with yellow flowers.
A. chantinii (Equatorial S. America). Leaves of olive-green, with vivid, contracting crossbands of pinkish-grey to white; inflorescence red tipped yellow.
A. coelestris 'Albo-marginata'. Grey-green leaves, variegated creamy-white. A red inflorescence with blue petals.
A. cylindrata (Brazil). Green leaves and magenta inflorescence with violet-blue petals.
A. fasciata (Brazil). Leaves, green-striped silver; inflorescence pink with blue and red.

Aechmea angustifolia

Aechmea 'Bert'

Aechmea bracteata

Aechmea caudata

Aechmea caudata variegata

Aechmea caudata variegata, wide-leaf form

Aechmea chantinii, Amazonian Zebra Plant

Aechmea coelestris 'Albo-marginata'

Aechmea cylindrata

Aechmea fasciata, Silver Vase

BROMELIADS, continued

A. fasciata **'Albo-marginata'.** Has a thin cream centre stripe.

A. fasciata purpurea (Brazil). Same habit and flower as A. Fasciata, but leaves are brown-purple banded with grey.

A. fasciata **'Silver King'*.** The leaves are almost entirely frosted silver; same inflorescence.

A. fasciata **'Variegata'.** The variegated-leaf form.

A. fosteriana (Brazil). A tall tube of yellow-green leaves, with deep brown irregular markings; spike of crimson, with yellow petals.

A. **'Fosters Favourite'.** Narrow rosette of glossy wine-red leaves; inflorescence a spike of coral-red pear-shaped berries with dark-blue flowers.

A. **'Fosters Favourite Favourite'.** The variegated form.

Aechmea fasciata variegata, Variegated Silver Vase

Aechmea 'Foster's Favourite'

Aechmea fosteriana

Aechmea fasciata 'Albo-marginata'

Aechmea fasciata purpurea

Aechmea 'Foster's Favourite Favourite'

68

A. gamosepala × cylindrata var. micrantha. Green leaves and pinkish inflorescence, with blue petals.

A. gracilis (Brazil). Green leaves. A branched inflorescence, red with blue petals.

A. lueddemanniana (S. America). Stiff rosette of metallic-green to bronze leaves; inflorescence is a panicle of white berries, turning purple-blue.

A. mariae-reginae (Costa Rica). Large plant, green flecked leaves. Large inflorescence with 15 cm flower head, pink bracts, and white and blue petals.

A. marmorata (S. Brazil). Correctly *Quesnelia marmorata*. Grecian Urn Plant. Tall blue-green tube, mottled green and maroon. Spike of rose-pink bracts and blue flowers.

A. mexicana (Mexico). Large plant with green mottled leaves, turning to rose. Erect rose and white flowers and pearl-like berries.

Aechmea lueddemanniana

Aechmea gamosepala × cylindrata var. *micrantha*

Aechmea mariae-reginae

Aechmea mexicana

Aechmea marmorata (Quesnelia marmorata)

Aechmea gracilis

BROMELIADS, continued

A. miniata discolor (Brazil). Leaves green with red reverse; inflorescence is a panicle of orange-red berries and blue flowers.

A. nudicaulis aureo-rosea* (S. Brazil). Leaves deep green; inflorescence of small red flowers.

A. nudicaulis cuspidata (Brazil). A stiff rosette, with black thorns; red bract and yellow flowers.

A. nudicaulis var. nudicaulis (S. Brazil). Stiff green leaves, black base and spines, red inflorescence, with yellow flowers.

A. orlandiana (Brazil). Leaves yellow-green cross-banded with brown; inflorescence of scarlet bracts and ivory flowers.

Aechmea nudicaulis var. *nudicaulis*

Aechmea nudicaulis cuspidata

Aechmea orlandiana

70   *Aechmea miniata discolor*

A. racinae (Brazil). Leaves shiny green; inflorescence, berry-like orange-red with yellow and black flowers.
A. ramosa (Brazil). Long green leaves, dusted silver and black spines. Red flower spike, with berry-like flowers. Long lasting.
A. recurvata (Brazil). Rosette of vase-shaped green leaves with spines; inflorescence, short flower-spike with shiny red bract and orchid-pink petals.
A. **'Royal Wine'.** Soft leaves, very glossy, of apple-green fully lacquered burgundy, red beneath; spike of orange berries with blue flowers.
A. weilbachii (Brazil). Coppery green leaves, red beneath and spined; inflorescence red, with mauve petals.

Aechmea racinae

Aechmea 'Royal Wine'

Aechmea weilbachii

Aechmea ramosa

Aechmea recurvata

BROMELIADS, continued

ANANAS
Pineapple

As well as growing any of the Pineapple varieties, it is often satisfying to grow tops from fruiting Pineapples you have purchased at your local fruit shop. Once broken off, these may be placed on top of a pot of soil. Eventually they will take root. I often place three tops in one pot, to make a more substantial display. Keep the wells full of water.

Light: Requires bright light to sun, indoors, or warmth and sun indoors, in order to fruit.
Water: Keep well full and soil moist.
Soil: Orchid Compost.
Fertiliser: Liquid fertiliser to the soil, monthly.
Propagation: Remove large off-shoots after fruiting, or grow tops.

Varieties include:
*A. bracteatus** (S. Brazil). The spines are larger and more widely spaced than *comosus*. Flower lavender, rougher fruit.
*A. bracteatus** **'Striatus'.** The variegated form.
A. comosus (Bahia). The commercial Pineapple. Has tough, spiny leaves, grey to bronze-green. A dense head of violet flower, followed by an edible pineapple.
A. comosus **'Variegatus'** (sp. Bahia). Variegated Pineapple, with boldly coloured leaves of deep green margined cream, tinted rosy red.

Ananas comosus variegatus – in fruit

Ananas comosus 'Variegatus', Variegated Pineapple

Ananas comosus – Fruiting pineapples grow from tops

BILLBERGIA

These attractive and usually tall Bromeliads are often beautifully banded. The flowers are highly colourful and well worth growing although unfortunately short-lived.

Light: Bright light to sun.
Water: Keep water in the well at all times, but keep the soil on the dry side. Mist foliage occasionally.
Soil: Orchid Compost.
Fertiliser: Liquid fertiliser to plant well (half strength) and to soil, monthly.
Propagation: Remove larger off-shoots after flowering.

Varieties include:
B. amoena (Brazil). Leaves grey-green, cross-banded with silver; inflorescence of rose bracts with green flowers edged with blue.
B. amoena rubra. Tall rosy-red tube, with white and yellow spots.
B. amoena rubra striatum. Similar, but more heavily spotted.
B. amoena viridis. Similar, with the green and rose foliage more vivid.
B. 'Catherine Wilson'. Small variety, nicely marked with cream and rose. The inflorescence is blue and green, with rose bracts.
B. elegans. Urn-shaped, attractive silver-green leaves, with spines; inflorescence, a branched spike with numerous rose bracts and long green flowers.

Billbergia elegans

Billbergia 'Catherine Wilson'

Billbergia amoena

Billbergia amoena rubra

Billbergia amoena rubra striatum

Billbergia amoena viridis

BROMELIADS, continued

B. euphemiae* (S. Brazil). Leaves grey-green, cross-banded with silver; inflorescence of rosy bracts with blue flowers.

B. 'Fantasia'. Leaves coppery green, heavily spotted creamy-white and pink; rose bract and blue flowers.

B. glenniana. Small purplish green leaves with cream spots. Red bracts with whitish-green and purple flowers.

B. horrida* var. *tigrina (sp. S. Brazil). The stiff, fluted leaves are purplish brown, banded with white; inflorescence red with spidery blue flowers.

B. leptopodia (Brazil). Permanent Wave Plant. Small pale green and silver leaves, which curl back on the ends, erect inflorescence of yellowish-green, tipped blue and with rose bracts.

B. macrocalyx (Brazil). Leaves green with silver bands; inflorescence of rosy bracts with large pale-blue flowers.

Billbergia glenniana

Billbergia macrocalyx

Billbergia 'Fantasia', Marbled Rainbow Plant

Billbergia leptopodia, Permanent Wave Plant

Billbergia horrida var. *tigrina*

74

B. **'Myee'**. The narrow rosy-red tube is heavily spotted with yellow.

B. *nutans** (S. Brazil). Fast-clumping narrow rosettes of silver-green leaves; inflorescence, a pink bract with green and violet flowers.

B. *pyramidalis concolour* (Brazil). A broad rosette of light-green leaves, resembling a bird's nest; inflorescence, a spectacular short-lived coral-red bract, with red flowers, tipped purple.

B. **pyramidalis var.** *pyramidalis* (Brazil). Leaves are bronze-green, with faint grey banding, inflorescence of purplish-red, with blue flowers.

B. *rosea* (Trinidad). Leaves tall, scurfy-grey, inflorescence of rosy bracts and yellow-green petals.

B. *saundersii* × *amoena*. Short rosette of pinkish-green leaves, spotted with cream; red petalled spike with green and blue flowers.

Billbergia pyramidalis var. *pyramidalis*

Billbergia pyramidalis concolour, Summer Torch

Billbergia rosea

Billbergia saundersii × *amoena*

BROMELIADS, continued

B. **'Theodore L. Mead'.** Spreading green tube with long-lasting, drooping inflorescence of blue and green, with rose bracts. Free-flowering.

B. **'Violet Beauty' var. red raven.** Handsome rosy-purple tube and open inflorescence of violet, with rose bracts.

B. windii. A small plant, olive-green, with faint bands of silver; inflorescence of red, with creamy-green corolla and blue petals.

B. zebrina (Central America). An attractive species with a tall rosette of purple-bronze leaves, heavily cross-banded with silvery white, and large black spines; inflorescence, a red bract with blue flowers.

BROMELIA

Bromelias somewhat resemble Pineapples. They are mostly large-growing, and very thorny. Best grown outdoors in the garden. They require filtered to bright sun, ample moisture and occasional liquid fertiliser.

Varieties include:

B. balansae (Brazil). Grows to about 1 m, in a rosette of thorny leaves. When ready to bloom the centre turns red, then the pink-bract flower head emerges, followed by an orange fruit.

Billbergia 'Violet Beauty' var. red raven

Billbergia 'Theodore L. Mead'

Billbergia windii

Billbergia zebrina, Zebra Urn

Bromelia balansae, Pinuela

CRYPTANTHUS
Star Bromeliad

These small star-shaped and horizontal bromeliads are often vividly banded. They grow quite well indoors, make attractive table plants, and because of their smaller size are very adaptable for terrariums.

Light: Bright light to filtered sun.
Water: Mist foliage regularly and keep soil dry between waterings. Likes humidity.
Soil: Orchid Compost.
Fertiliser: Use liquid fertiliser on soil monthly, and occasionally use foliar fertiliser over foliage.
Propagation: Plant larger suckers as they fall from plant.

Varieties include:
*C. acaulis ruber** (Brazil). A small plant with bronze, horizontal, stiff leaves, covered with beige scurf; inflorescence white.
C. artley. Delicate shading from cream to pink with blackish bands.
C. bahianus (Bahia). Stiff, narrow leaves, with wavy saw edge, apple-green, with margins turning bronzy-red; white flowers.
C. bivittatus lueddemannii (Brazil). Thicker, smooth, wavy-edged leaves, bright pink, with two bands of pale green; white flowers.
*C. bivittatus minor** (Brazil). Small, flattened, star-like variety with olive-green leaves, striped pink.
C. bivittatus **'Pink Starlight'.** Beautiful bands of blackish-green, cream and pink to red.
C. bromeliodes tricolour (Brazil). A striking variety, its green and ivory variegated leaves beautifully marked with pink.
*C. beuckeri** (Brazil). Rosette of pale-green leaves, shaded and mottled deeper green and pink; white flowers.

Cryptanthus bivittatus 'Pink Starlight'

Cryptanthus bromeliodes tricolour, Rainbow Star

Cryptanthus bivittatus lueddemannii

Cryptanthus bahianus

Cryptanthus artley

BROMELIADS, continued

C. **'Cascade'.** Wavy variety, in shades of green with brown shading.
C. **'Costers Favourite'.** Colourful bands of red and black.
C. diversifolius (Brazil). Broader saw-toothed leaves, fawn-green, covered in grey scurf; white flowers.
C. fosterianus (Brazil). Larger and more vivid than 'Zebrinus' with coppery-green, to purplish-brown leaves, with tan zebra banding.
C. **'Green Ice'.** Vivid green to silver.

Cryptanthus 'Cascade'

Cryptanthus fosterianus, Stiff Pheasant Leaf

Cryptanthus diversifolius, Vary-leaf Star

Cryptanthus 'Coster's Favourite'

Cryptanthus 'Green Ice'

Cryptanthus 'Mars'

C. × **'It'**. Vivid stripes of red, cream, and green, becoming suffused with pink.

C. **'Mars'**. Saw-toothed leaves, bronze-red, with centre margin of pale green, small amount of white scurf; white flowers.

C. osyanus. Broad, saw-toothed leaves, blending from pale green to pink and coppery red; white flowers.

C. × *rubescens**. A low rosette of wavy, purplish-bronze leaves, covered with fine silvery scurf.

C. zebra. Deep blackish-green leaves vividly edged in cream.

C. zonatus (Brazil). A small plant with brownish-green scaly leaves cross-banded tan to light brown.

C. zonatus zebrinus. Another striking form, with bronzy-purple leaves, cross-banded with silvery-beige.

Cryptanthus zonatus zebrinus, Zebra Plant

Cryptanthus zonatus

Cryptanthus × 'It', colour band

Cryptanthus zebra

Cryptanthus × *osyanus*

79

BROMELIADS, continued

CRYPTBERGIA

A hybrid of Cryptanthus and Billbergia. Taller growing than Cryptanthus, and useful for pots or hanging pots; hardy enough to tolerate some neglect.

Light: Needs bright light or full sun to retain best colour.
Water: Mist foliage regularly, but allow soil to dry between waterings.
Soil: Orchid Compost.
Fertiliser: Use liquid fertiliser on soil, monthly, and occasionally apply foliar fertiliser over foliage.
Propagation: Best to divide clusters occasionally.

Varieties include:
C. × meadii (Crypt. beuckeri × Billb. nutans). A short plant with a rosette of pale green, mottled deeper, leaves, sometimes with a coppery flush; short inflorescence, pink with green flowers.

GUZMANIA

Guzmanias are especially prized for their glossy leaves with colourful patterns, in addition to their long-lasting inflorescence.

Light: Medium to low light, but brighter indoors.
Water: Keep water in the well and soil slightly damp.
Soil: Orchid Compost.
Fertiliser: Foliar, at half strength, monthly.
Propagation: By large sucker or division, or from seed.

Varieties include:
G. lingulata minor (Central America). Yellowish-green leaves and yellow to red inflorescence and whitish-yellow flowers.
G. vittata (Colombia, Brazil). Beautiful green leaves cross-banded in silver, insignificant inflorescence with white flowers.

Guzmania lingulata minor

Cryptbergia × meadii

Guzmania vittata

NEOREGELIA
Blushing Bromeliads

Among the most colourful of Bromeliads. They have beautiful, smooth, shining leaves, which develop colourful centre formations, with the flower heads down inside the wells.

Light: Best allowed to colour up in bright light to filtered sun, then taken indoors, to a bright position.
Water: Mist foliage regularly, and keep centre well full at all times. Keep soil moist, not over-wet.
Soil: Orchid Compost.
Fertiliser: Use liquid fertiliser on soil, monthly. Occasionally use foliar fertiliser over foliage and to well at half strength.
Propagation: Best to divide matured plants, after they have clustered and firmed up.

Varieties include:
N. ampullacea. Has a dwarf tube, about 15 cm high, of dark-green leaves with brown markings. Propagates on thin rhizomes about 8 cm long, and rapidly forms a clump; a small head of blue flowers, within the tube.
N. ampullacea **'Tigrina'*.** The yellow-green leaves are more boldly marked.
N. bahiana viridis* (Brazil). A low and shapely rosette of pea-green, glossy leaves, clumps rapidly, white flowers.
N. carolinae (Brazil). The green leaves are bright red in the centre of the rosette-shaped plant; inflorescence is pincushion-like, with purple and white petals.
N. carolinae **'Marechalii'.** Shorter, broader with rose coloured centre.
N. carolinae **'Meyendorffii'** (Brazil). The olive-green leaves have coppery tinting, and turn maroon in the centre at flowering time; the pincushion inflorescence has lilac petals.
N. carolinae **'Tricolour'** (Brazil). An attractive variety, with the glossy green leaves striped ivory-white, and tinted pink, later the whole centre of the plant turns carmine-red; centre flowers of blue.

Neoregelia ampullacea

Neoregelia carolinae, Blushing Bromeliad

Neoregelia carolinae 'Meyendorffii'

Neoregelia carolinae 'Marechalii'

Neoregelia carolinae 'Tricolour', Striped Blushing Bromeliad

BROMELIADS, continued

N. concentrica (Brazil). Leaves are green with purple blotches; when in flower the centre turns purple-red; the pincushion inflorescence has blue petals.

N. concentrica **'Red Nest'.** Similar, with a vivid reddish-purple colouring.

N. concentrica variegata. This is handsomely edged with cream.

N. cruenta × spectabilis. The bronzy-green leaves have purple-red tips, and are silverish beneath.

N. **'Fireball'.** The pale green leaves eventually become glossy, purplish-red all over. Also called 'Schultziana' and 'Red of Rio'.

N. × **'Jodie' var. 'Gay Rebel'.** The pale green leaves turn dull purple-red.

Neoregelia concentrica variegata

Neoregelia concentrica 'Red Nest'

Neoregelia cruenta × spectabilis

Neoregelia 'Jodie' var. 'Gay Rebel'

Neoregelia concentrica

Neoregelia 'Fireball'

Neoregelia olwen ferris var. 'Magenta'

Neoregelia 'Magna'

Neoregelia 'Little Gem'

Neoregelia tristis

N. **'Little Gem'.** Small plant, turning vivid purple-red, in good light.

N. **'Magna'.** The pale green leaves become flushed with purple red.

N. marmorata hybrid* (Brazil). A bold rosette with urn-shaped deep-red leaves, spotted with yellowish-green; the central inflorescence has blue flowers.

N. olwen ferris **var. 'Magenta'.** Vivid green leaves, with black spines and reddish-purple centre.

N. punctatissima (Brazil). Small and free-suckering, green banded bronze and black.

N. sarmentosa* (Brazil). A medium-sized rosette of broad olive-green leaves, the base of which is deep brown, reducing to spots further up the leaves; inflorescence, a large head of pale blue flowers.

N. sarmentosa chlorostricta (Rio de Janeiro). Small rosette of purplish-red leaves, spotted green, white flowers, suckers above the ground.

N. spectabilis (Brazil). Fingernail Plant. Leaves are olive-green tipped with pink, underside banded grey; pincushion inflorescence has blue petals.

N. tristis (Brazil). Green to grey-green leaves, mottled purplish-maroon and red tipped.

Neoregelia sarmentosa chlorostricta

Neoregelia punctatissima

Neoregelia spectabilis, Fingernail Plant

83

BROMELIADS, continued

NEOTANTHUS
(Neoregelia × Cryptanthus)

An interesting hybrid cross, with characteristics of both parents. Many more interesting varieties should emerge, as further hybridization is carried out.

Varieties include:

N. × **'Cardboard'.** The foliage has an unusual texture. Blue flowers.
N. × **'Waffle'.** The glossy-green foliage has an unusual banding in purple and paler green. Still to flower.

Neotanthus × 'Waffle'

Neotanthus × 'Cardboard'

NIDULARIUM
Bird's Nest Bromeliads

Nidulariums are very similar to Neoregelias, but not as hardy or vigorous. However, they are just as adaptable to indoor conditions.

Light: Bright light to filtered sun, but are more tolerant of poorer light than other Bromeliads.
Water: Keep well full, and soil moist but not over-wet. Mist foliage regularly for added humidity.
Soil: Orchid Compost.
Fertiliser: Use liquid fertiliser to soil monthly, and foliar fertiliser at half strength over foliage, occasionally.
Propagation: Best to divide plants, after the suckers have grown larger and harder.

Varieties include:

N. fulgens (S.E. Brazil). Leaves are bright green with dark mottling; centre cup bright crimson; flowers blue.
N. innocentii **var.** *innocentii* (Brazil). The green leaves become deep purple, almost black. Rusty-red centre with white flowers.
N. innocentii **'Lineatum'** (Brazil). A rosette of green leaves heavily striped white; inflorescence is a centre rosette of red leaves.
N. innocentii striatum (Brazil). This variety differs from the above in that the stripes are creamy-white, and in the centre only; red centre inflorescence.
N. innocentii viridis. Pale green leaves, centre tipped red, with white flowers.

Nidularium fulgens, Blushing Cup

Nidularium innocentii var. *innocentii*,
Black Amazonian Bird's Nest·

PORTEA

P. petropolitana extensa (Brazil). This taller-growing Bromeliad is quite striking, with its tall flower spike (around 1.5 m) in red and blue, and contrasting glossy green leaves.

Light: Best grown outdoors (warm) or in glasshouse or bush-house and taken indoors to flower. Light should be bright to filtered sun. Sunroom is ideal.
Water: Keep well full and mist foliage regularly. Keep soil moderately dry.
Soil: Orchid Compost.
Fertiliser: Use liquid fertiliser to the soil monthly, and foliar fertiliser over the foliage occasionally.
Propagation: Divide matured clusters.

Nidularium innocentii viridis

Nidularium innocentii 'Lineatum',
Lined Bird's Nest

Portea petropolitana extensa

*Nidularium
innocentii striatum*

85

BROMELIADS, continued

TILLANDSIA
Airplant Bromeliads

These are the most unusual of Bromeliads, and are tree-top plants in their natural environment. They are very much at home when attached by a ball of sphagnum moss to poles and larger trees, in warm temperatures. Some may be potted and adapt to indoor conditions. Good in lit terrariums.

Light: Bright light to filtered sun.
Water: These are humidity-loving and should be regularly misted over the foliage, especially during summer. If the plants are in soil, this should be kept dryish. If attached in moss, this should also be induced to dry out between waterings.
Soil: Orchid Compost.
Fertiliser: Use liquid fertiliser to soil, or foliar fertiliser monthly.
Propagation: Divide clustered matured plants, occasionally.

Varieties include:
*T. brachycaulis** (Central America). Small rosette of stiff, recurving green leaves, red at flowering time; small head of violet flowers.
T. cyanea (Ecuador). Small rosette of stiff, brownish-green leaves; flattened pink flower bract, with violet butterfly-like flowers.
T. fasciculata (Florida to Central America). Grey-green leaves and erect flower spike green tinged red, blue flowers.
T. flabellata (Central America). Short grey-green leaves, spreading flower heads of scarlet with violet-blue petals.
T. tricolour (Mexico to Costa Rica). Grey-green leaves, erect red spike with violet petals, from either side.
T. usneoides (Central to S. America). Spanish Moss. Thread-like strands of silver-grey, hangs like moss. Air-growing for glasshouse, warm bush-house, or trees, etc.

Tillandsia tricolour

Tillandsia cyanea, Pink Quill

Tillandsia flabellata

Tillandsia fasciculata

Tillandsia usneoides, Spanish Moss

VRIESEA
Flaming Sword

Vrieseas have either shiny green or beautifully banded, glossy foliage, and long-lasting, very attractive flower spikes, in the most brilliant of shades, between red and yellow. They are most adaptable as indoor plants. Good in lit terrariums.

Light: Moderate to bright light preferred.
Water: Keep wells full at all times and moisten foliage frequently; however soil should be kept on the dry side.
Soil: Orchid Compost.
Fertiliser: Use liquid fertiliser to the soil monthly, and foliar fertiliser over the foliage, occasionally.
Propagation: By seeds, or divide mature clusters.

Varieties include:
V. Belgian hybrid × schwackeana. Small plant with erect spike of yellow shaded in red, yellow flowers.
V. bituminosa* (Brazil). Leaves are blue-green tipped with purple; flower spike of bracts with yellow flowers.
V. carinata (S.E. Brazil). Painted Feather. A low pale-green rosette of leaves; inflorescence, a flattened feather-like bract, deep yellow with crimson centre, yellow flowers.
V. ensiformis (Brazil). Leaves pale green tipped with purple; flower spike of red bracts and yellow flowers.
V. × erecta. Green leaves with erect spike of vivid red, with yellow flowers.
V. erythrodactylon (S.E. Brazil). Leaves pale green; flower spike with coxcomb-like head of greenish bracts, tipped with pink.
V. flammea (S. Brazil). Narrow leaves and long, thin spike, with open red bracts and white petals. Clustering habit.
V. fenestralis* (Brazil). A showy high rosette of yellow-green leaves, cross-lined in deep green, purplish beneath; yellow flower spike.

Vriesea erythrodactylon   *Vriesea erecta*

Vriesea ensiformis (at rear) and *Vriesea erecta* (in front)

Vriesea flammea   *Vriesea carinata,* Painted Feather or Lobster Claw   *Vriesea Belgian hybrid × schwackeana*

BROMELIADS, continued

V. gigantea (tessellata) (S.E. Brazil). Broad leaves are bluish-green with darker checker-board markings and purple edging and tips; flower spike with green bracts and yellow flowers.

V. hieroglyphica (S.E. Brazil). A beautifully marked variety with broad yellow-green leaves, cross-banded with hieroglyphic markings, deep green above and purple beneath; flower spike with yellow flowers.

V. incurvata (S.E. Brazil). Leaves light green; flower spike with red bract edged with yellow, and yellow flowers.

V. petropolitana (Brazil). A compact rosette of green leaves, flushed with red; the short orange bract resembles a plump goldfish. Syn. *V. heterostachys.*

V. petropolitana × erythrodactylon. A soft rosette of pale green leaves in the centre, purplish-red backed in the lower; inflorescence a yellow and red bract, with yellow flowers.

V. philippo-coburgii (Brazil). A handsome rosette of soft-green leaves, black at the base of the plant; yellow and red bract with yellow flowers.

Vriesea hieroglyphica, King of Bromeliads

Vriesea petropolitana × erythrodactylon

Vriesea petropolitana

Vriesea incurvata, Sidewinder Vriesea

Vriesea gigantea (tessellata)

Vriesea philippo-coburgii,
Vagabond Plant

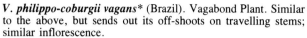

*V. philippo-coburgii vagans** (Brazil). Vagabond Plant. Similar to the above, but sends out its off-shoots on travelling stems; similar inflorescence.

V. platynema (W. Indies, Brazil). Broad green leaves have wavy-line markings and purple flush. Floral bracts are reddish with white petals.

V. procera (Brazil). Rosette of pale green leaves, tinted with light brown. A flat flower spike, about 30 cm long, yellow marked red.

V. recurvata (Brazil). Soft green leaves and pendant spike of yellow and red, with yellow petals.

V. regina (Brazil). Leaves waxy-green heavily speckled with maroon dots; an extremely tall flower spike with pink bracts and creamy flowers.

V. 'Rex'. Green leaves, long garnet-red flower bract with yellow petals.

V. rodigasiana × ensiformis. Rosette of pale-green leaves; tall branching spike of yellow and red, with yellow flowers.

Vriesea rodigasiana × ensiformis

Vriesea recurvata   *Vriesea procera*   *Vriesea regina*

Vriesea platynema   *Vriesea 'Rex'*

BROMELIADS, continued

V. saundersii (Rio de Janeiro). A small, stiff rosette of grey, spotted purple-red; arching branched spike of lemon-yellow, with yellow flowers.

*V. scalaris** (Brazil). A small compact rosette of coppery leaves; inflorescence, a pendant red bract, with yellow flowers.

V. schwackeana (S. Brazil). Sturdy dull-green leaves spotted maroon. Tall branched lasting flower spike of rich red with yellow petals.

V. splendens **'Major'**. Flaming Sword. This beautifully marked variety has a broad rosette of bluish-green leaves, heavily cross-banded with purple markings; inflorescence, a tall, flattened, fiery-red, long-lasting spike, with yellow flowers.

WITTROCKIA (Syn. *Nidularium amazonica*)

W. smithii (Brazil). A medium-sized variety with broad, thin, dark red leaves. A sunken inflorescence in white and green. It is generally grown outdoors in filtered sun, in Orchid Compost, and allowed to dry between waterings.

Vriesea splendens major,
Flaming Sword

Vriesea saundersii

Vriesea schwackeana

Wittrockia smithii (Nidularium amazonica)

BROWALLIA   Solanaceae

Amethyst Flower

A continuous flowering plant, which is occasionally sold as
an indoor pot plant.

Grow: In glasshouse or warm bush-house.
Position indoors: Grow in sunroom or near bright window.
Filtered sun.
Water: Keep evenly moist, preferably immerse pot.
Soil: Indoor Potting Mix.
Fertiliser: Complete Plant Food (liquid or foliar) every 3–4
weeks.
Propagation: From seed or cuttings.
Pests and problems: Regularly start fresh plants.

Varieties include:
B. speciosa major (Colombia). Spreading plant, with deep green
leaves and masses of violet blue flowers. There is also a white
variety.

CALADIUM   Araceae

Angel Wings

These colourful, tuberous, tropical plants are much prized
as indoor and glasshouse specimens. Like Alocasias, they
are winter-dormant, and require the pots to be kept dry, in
an effort to save the warmth-loving bulbs.

Grow: In tropical, sheltered gardens or in pots in
glasshouses. In temperate garden corners and on patios.
Position indoors: Ideal in sunrooms or near bright
windows.
Water: Require frequent waterings to keep damp. Dry off
at dormancy.
Soil: Indoor Potting Mix.
Fertiliser: Complete Plant Food (dry, liquid, or foliar).
Propagation: From seeds or dividing larger tubers.
Pests and problems: Watch for spider mites.

Varieties include:
C. bicolour (Trop. America). Fancy-leafed Caladiums. Tuberous
plants producing beautifully marked, and often transparent, leaf
patterns in red, pink and white on green. Many are heavily veined.
Continual hybridisation has produced many highly coloured and
beautiful leaf designs, many of which have been given variety
names. A selection has been pictured.

Caladium bicolour, Fancy Leaf Caladium

Browallia speciosa major, Amethyst Flower

Caladium bicolour, Fancy Leaf Caladium

Caladium bicolour, Fancy Leaf
Caladium

91

CALCEOLARIA Scrophulariaceae

Pocket Book Plant

These colourful pot plants, with the pouch-like flowers, are widely used in park greenhouse displays, but can also be used to brighten your home.

Grow: In cool glasshouses, bush-houses, or on sheltered verandah.
Position indoors: Shaded sunroom or near bright, cool window.
Water: Allow to dry between watering.
Soil: Indoor Potting Mix.
Fertiliser: Complete Plant Food (dry, liquid, or foliar).
Propagation: From seeds or cuttings.
Pests and problems: After flowering has finished, discard and start fresh plants.

Varieties include:
C. herbeohybrida **'Grandiflora'.** (Chile). Beautiful pot plants with thin fresh-green leaves and clusters of showy pouch-type flowers in shades of yellow to red, often spotted red and flowering in spring. Also adaptable for basket growing.
C. herbeohybrida **'Multiflora nana'.** A dwarf strain, very adaptable for pot growing, and has smaller flowers.

CEROPEGIA Asclepiadaceae

Rosary Vine

A hanging plant producing numerous, slender trails hanging to 1 m or more. Commonly called Rosary Vine, or Chain of Hearts. Excellent outdoors or indoors, and quite easily grown.

Grow: In hanging pots under trees, on patios, bush-houses or glasshouses. Filtered sun.
Position indoors: Sunroom or near bright window. Filtered sun or bright light.
Water: Allow to dry between waterings.
Soil: Indoor Potting Mix.
Fertiliser: Complete Plant Food (dry, liquid, or foliar).
Propagation: From cutting or by division.
Pests and problems: Few.

Varieties include:
C. barkleyi (S. Africa). This variety differs only from *C. woodii* in its narrower, pointed leaves.
C. debilis (Malawi). The long, pedulous, thread-like stems have small, narrow leaves and greenish flowers, marked with purple.
C. woodii (Natal). String of Hearts or Rosary Vine. Fine, thread-like stem and small heart-shaped leaves in pairs; flowers are purplish.

Calceolaria herbeohybrida 'Grandiflora', Pocket Book Plant

Calceolaria herbeohybrida 'Multiflora Nana', Dwarf Pocket Book Plant

Ceropegia barkleyi

CHLORANTHUS   Chloranthaceae

Fairy Tears

Small spill-over or hanging plant which grows well indoors, even tolerating poor light.

Grow: In glasshouse or summer bush-house. Filtered sun to good light.
Position indoors: Sunroom or reasonable light position indoors.
Water: Keep moist, requires regular watering.
Soil: Indoor Potting Mix.
Fertiliser: Complete Plant Food (dry, liquid, or foliar) monthly.
Propagation: From cuttings.
Pests and problems: Mealy bugs.

Varieties include:
C. spicatus (**inconspicuous**) (China). Oval, serrated-edged leaf of deep, shiny green. The heads of flower buds form on the ends of all shoots in spring to autumn and open into small yellow berries which soon fall, but are attractive while they last.

Chloranthus spicatus (inconspicuous), Fairy Tears

Ceropegia woodii, Rosary Vine or String of Hearts

93

CISSUS   Vitaceae

Grape Ivy

A popular series of creepers hardy for indoor use, and widely grown throughout the world. Known as Grape Ivy, Kangaroo Vine and Idiot-Proof Plant. They attach to supports by tendrils.

Grow: Glasshouse or warm bush-house.
Position indoors: Sunroom or near bright window. Bright to filtered sun.
Water: Keep moist.
Soil: Indoor Potting Mix.
Fertiliser: Complete Plant Food (dry, liquid, or foliar) monthly.
Propagation: From cuttings.
Pests and problems: Mealy bugs and spider mites.

Varieties include:
C. antarctica (Australia). Kangaroo vine. Deep-green foliage, serrated edge; slow creeper.
C. discolour (Java). Rex Begonia Vine. A colourful creeper with heart-shaped, velvety, moss-green leaves, spotted silvery-white and maroon beneath; red stems. Requires more warmth. Winter dormant. Prefers a sunroom.
C. rhombifolia (W. Indies, N. and S. America). Grape Ivy. A fast growing, twining vine, very adaptable indoors, given fair light.
C. rhombifolia **'Ellen Danica'.** An attractive Danish introduction, with more segmented, oak-shaped leaves.
C. rotundifolia. Idiot-Proof Plant, or Arabian Wax Cissus. Easily grown and has round, heavy, brittle, glossy leaves.

Cissus rhombifolia 'Ellen Danica'

Cissus discolour, Rex Begonia Vine

Cissus antarctica, Kangaroo Vine

Cissus rotundifolia, Idiot-proof Plant or Arabian Wax Cissus

Cissus rhombifolia, Grape Ivy

94

CLERODENDRUM   Verbenaceae

Bleeding Hearts

This tropical family contains both shrubs and creepers, each with attractive flowers. Popular as glasshouse, bush-house, and indoor plants.

Grow: Glasshouse and warm bush-house, sheltered patio.
Position indoors: Airy sunroom or near a bright airy window.
Water: Keep evenly moist.
Soil: Indoor Potting Mix.
Fertiliser: Complete Plant Food (dry, liquid, or foliar) monthly during growing period.
Propagation: From cuttings.
Pests and problems: None in particular. Short periods indoors, then rotate.

Varieties include:
C. fragrans plentiflorum (China, Japan). Glory Tree. A shrubby plant with large, hairy leaves and a cluster of fully double, beautifully fragrant, white flowers, flushed mauve.
C. splendens (S.E. Asia). A vigorous creeper for warm positions outdoors, or in a glasshouse; dark-green foliage; clusters of dark-red flowers during summer and autumn.
C. thompsonae (Africa). Bleeding Heart. A twining plant with showy clusters of crimson flowers with white bracts which turn pink.

Clerodendrum thompsonae, Bleeding Heart Vine

Clerodendrum fragrans plentiflorum, Glory Tree

Clerodendrum splendens

CODIAEUM Euphorbiaceae

Croton

Crotons are widely sought after, for their brilliantly coloured foliage. Besides their tropical garden appeal, they have become one of the most popular pot plants for warm patios, poolsides, and indoors. It is quite common if touring Queensland to see cut sections of Crotons taking root indoors in vases of water. These days new varieties suitable for indoor growing are appearing on the market.

Grow: In warm gardens, warm patios, bush-houses (over 25°C) and glasshouses. Bright sun.
Position indoors: Bright sunroom or near sunny window.
Water: Evenly moist.
Soil: General Potting Mix.
Fertiliser: Complete Plant Food (dry, liquid, or foliar) monthly during growing period.
Propagation: From cuttings.
Pests and problems: Spider mites.

Varieties include:
C. variegatum pictum (S. India, Sri Lanka, Malaya). With constant hybridising, and natural pollination, many brilliant and colourful varieties are emerging. Only brilliantly coloured pictures can portray the following range of named varieties.
C. v.p. **'Andreanum'.** Matured leaves are blackish-green, veined with red; juvenile leaves are fresh green, veined with yellow.
C. v.p. **'Anthony Hordern'*.** Bronze-green leaves occasionally variegated with orange-red; juvenile leaves fresh green marked with yellow.
C. aucubaefolium. Smallish bright-green leaves liberally spotted with yellow.
C. v.p. **'Baronne de Rothschild'.** Oval leaves, olive-green with yellow, changing to orange and crimson; veins pink to red.
C. v.p. **'B'Comte'*.** Bronze-green leaves occasionally variegated with red; juvenile leaves, green marked with yellow.
C. v.p. **'Bicolour'.** The green leaves are spotted and shaded with cream, later pink and red.
C. v.p. **'Black Prince'*.** The oval leaves are deep, blackish-green only occasionally speckled red or orange.
C. v.p. **'Blair's Seedling'.** Long, narrow, recurving, blackish leaves, lightly striped margin and centre splashed with deep red; juvenile leaves green marked with yellow.

Codiaeum (Croton) variegatum pictum 'Baronne de Rothschild'

Codiaeum (Croton) aucubaefolium

Codiaeum (Croton) variegatum pictum 'Andreanum'

Codiaeum (Croton) variegatum pictum 'Blair's Seedling'

Codiaeum (Croton) variegatum pictum 'Bicolour'

Codiaeum (Croton) variegatum pictum 'Cairns Pink'

C. v.p. **'Brilliantissima'.** Large, floppy, mostly orange leaves marked with deep green and red; juvenile leaves green splashed with yellow.

C. v.p. **'Burnt Orange'.** Large, narrow, recurving leaves blackish, with a centre marking of orange spreading from the veins; juvenile leaves reddish-green.

C. v.p. **'Burtonii'.** Deep green, blotched yellow, later shading red.

C. v.p. **'Cairns Pink'.** Bronze leaves with a centre marking of pink and orange-red; juvenile leaves green with a cream centre.

C. v.p. **'Captain Kidd'.** A nice variety, having its deep-green leaves mottled with yellow, orange, and red.

Codiaeum (Croton) variegatum pictum 'Brilliantissima'

Codiaeum (Croton) variegatum pictum 'Captain Kidd'

Codiaeum (Croton) variegatum pictum 'Burnt Orange'

Codiaeum (Croton) variegatum pictum 'Burtonii'

CODIAEUM, continued

C. v.p. **'Cleopatra'.** Colourful, with the blackish leaves overlaid with cream to red.

C. v.p. **'Cornutum'.** An unusually shaped leaf, its midrib continuing beyond the end of the oval leaf; yellow midrib and markings.

C. v.p. **'Corsair'*.** Long narrow deep-green leaves spotted with yellow above and orange beneath.

C. v.p. **'Craigii'.** A horned leaf of deep green, heavily veined and spotted yellow.

C v.p. **'Delicatissimum'.** Long narrow deep-green leaves have a bright-red centre vein; juvenile leaves are veined in yellow.

C. v.p. **'Duke of Albany'.** Red-bronze leaves have a centre variegation, from the veins of creamy pink and red; juvenile leaves green with cream to pink variegation.

C. v.p. **'Duke of Windsor'.** Lobed, deep-green leaves marked with orange and red.

C. v.p. **'Edmontense'.** Narrow, wavy leaves are bronze, and marked with red veins and splashes; the vein continues from the end of the leaf; juvenile leaves green.

Codiaeum (Croton) variegatum pictum 'Delicatissimum'

Codiaeum (Croton) variegatum pictum 'Craigii'

Codiaeum (Croton) variegatum pictum 'Edmontense'

Codiaeum (Croton) variegatum pictum 'Cornutum'

Codiaeum (Croton) variegatum pictum 'Duke of Albany'

Codiaeum (Croton) variegatum pictum 'Duke of Windsor'

Codiaeum (Croton) variegatum pictum 'Cleopatra'

98

C. v.p. **'Elegantissima'.** Large floppy leaves, mostly yellow to orange, and deep green between the veins; juvenile leaves green splashed with yellow.

C. v.p. **'Eugene Drap'.** Deep green leaves heavily veined yellow.

C. v.p. **'Fitzroy Superba'.** Deep green leaves heavily overlaid yellow, flushing red later.

C. v.p. **'Flame Dance'.** Bronze-green leaves heavily veined in red; juvenile leaves green to bronze, with light-green to red veining.

C. v.p. **'Gloriosa'.** Colourful, with green and cream leaves changing to red and purplish black with age.

C. v.p. **'Golden Ring'***. Very narrow leaves are cream towards the yellow stems, and green at the ends.

C. v.p. **'Golden Shower'.** Long, narrow, sometimes spiralled, green leaves with a variegation of cream; the veins protrude from the ends of the leaves.

Codiaeum (Croton) variegatum pictum 'Eugene Drap'

Codiaeum (Croton) variegatum pictum 'Golden Shower'
with *Dracaena honoriae*

Codiaeum (Croton) variegatum pictum 'Fitzroy Superba'

Codiaeum (Croton) variegatum pictum
'Elegantissima'

Codiaeum (Croton) variegatum pictum 'Gloriosa'

Codiaeum (Croton) variegatum pictum
'Flame Dance'

99

CODIAEUM, continued

C. v.p. **'Goldfinger'.** A long, narrow leaf, broader at base, deep green, spotted and blotched golden yellow.

C. v.p. **'Graciosum'.** Graceful, long and very narrow, deep green leaves with blotches of yellow.

C. v.p. **'Hookerianum'*.** Glossy bright and blackish-green leaves with an unusual cream centre-marking.

C. v.p. **'Imperialis'.** A colourful mixture of green, black, and cream overlaid red and pink.

C. v.p. **'Indian Headdress'.** Erect leaves of green, black, and cream, overlaid orange and red.

C. v.p. **'Interruptum'.** Bronze-green leaves, oval at the base, with an inch or so of vein, then continuing to a long, narrow leaf; occasional red splashing; juvenile leaves green.

C. v.p. **'Jacob's Coat'.** The green leaves are heavily veined cream then orange, and red.

C. v.p. **'Joseph's Coat'.** As above, but of course the brighter of the two.

C. v.p. **'Katonii'*.** Heavily lobed dull-green leaves spotted in yellow.

Codiaeum (Croton) variegatum pictum 'Graciosum'

Codiaeum (Croton) variegatum pictum 'Goldfinger'

Codiaeum (Croton) variegatum pictum 'Interruptum'

Codiaeum (Croton) variegatum pictum 'Joseph's Coat'

Codiaeum (Croton) variegatum pictum 'Indian Headdress'

Codiaeum (Croton) variegatum pictum 'Imperialis'

Codiaeum (Croton) variegatum pictum 'Jacob's Coat'

C. v.p. **'King George'***. Broad, light-green leaves heavily veined in yellow, turning to red.

C. v.p. **'Lobatum'***. Broadly-lobed leaves, veined in yellow.

C. v.p. **'Madame Buffer'***. Narrow blackish leaves with a centre stripe of red; juvenile leaves fresh green, with lighter veins.

C. v.p. **'Magnifica'**. Large bright-green leaves heavily marked and veined in cream and yellow.

C. v.p. **'Magnolaefolia'**. Oval spoon-shaped bronze-green leaves marked with orange-red; juvenile leaves green splashed with cream.

C. v.p. **'Magnolaefolia' sport***. Oval deep-green leaves marbled with yellow and orange; red edge; juvenile leaves green splashed with cream.

C. v.p. **'Melrose Red'**. Green and black, with cream, overlaid orange and red.

C. v.p. **'Melville Red'**. Bronze leaves marked with pinkish-red; juvenile leaves deep green, marked with yellow to orange.

C. v.p. **'Mona Lisa'**. Large green leaf, with cream centre, ageing to black and yellow flushed red.

C. v.p. **'Monstrose'***. An unusually lobed variety, with green leaves sparingly marked with cream.

C. v.p. **'Mortii'**. A sturdy grower with waxy, long, oblong forest-green leaves with yellow veins and border, well defined.

Codiaeum (Croton) variegatum pictum 'Magnifica'

Codiaeum (Croton) variegatum pictum 'Magnolaefolia'

Codiaeum (Croton) variegatum pictum 'Melville Red'

Codiaeum (Croton) variegatum pictum 'Mona Lisa'

Codiaeum (Croton) variegatum pictum 'Melrose Red'

Codiaeum (Croton) variegatum pictum 'Mortii'

101

CODIAEUM, continued

C. v.p. **'Mrs. Iceton'.** Oval blackish-green leaves heavily marked between the veins with red and deep pink; juvenile leaves marked with cream.

C. v.p. **'Mrs. Sanders'.** (Fred Sanders). Deep-green, heavily lobed leaves have a large variegation of yellow; juvenile leaves fresh green marked with cream.

C. v.p. **'Nestar'.** The deep green leaves are centre-striped and spotted in cream.

C. v.p. **'Norma'.** New introduction, supposed to be indoor hardy, beautifully variegated leaves of green, black, and purple overlaid with cream, orange, and red.

C. v.p. **'Northern Queen'*.** Deep-green leaves, heavily veined and edged in yellow, with pinkish beneath showing through; juvenile leaves fresh green marked with cream.

C. v.p. **'Norwood Beauty'.** The green to blackish leaves are colourfully variegated with yellow, red, and orange.

Codiaeum (Croton) variegatum pictum 'Norwood Beauty'

Codiaeum (Croton) variegatum pictum 'Mrs Sanders'

Codiaeum (Croton) variegatum pictum 'Nestar'

Codiaeum (Croton) variegatum pictum 'Mrs Iceton'

Codiaeum (Croton) variegatum pictum 'Norma'

C. v.p. **'Prince of Wales'.** Narrow deep green, with centre stripe and spotting of yellow.

C. v.p. **'Princess Mary'.** Thin and twisted green to black leaves, with a centre band of yellow to red.

C. v.p. **'Punctatum Aureum'*.** Numerous very narrow deep-green leaves, heavily spotted in yellow.

C. v.p. **'Recurvatum'.** Narrow, recurving, deep-green leaves veined in cream.

C. v.p. **'Reidii'.** This beautiful variety has its large, broad, blackish leaves veined in deep red, contrasting with the fresh-green juvenile leaves, which are veined in yellow, tinged with pink.

Codiaeum (Croton) variegatum pictum 'Princess Mary'

Codiaeum (Croton) variegatum pictum 'Recurvatum'

Codiaeum (Croton) variegatum pictum 'Reidii' sport

Codiaeum (Croton) variegatum pictum 'Reidii'

Codiaeum (Croton) variegatum pictum 'Prince of Wales'

CODIAEUM, continued

C. v.p. **'Ribbonite'***. Long narrow deep-green leaves become heavily splashed with yellow, some almost entirely yellow.

C. v.p. **'Rising Sun'**. Oval leaves, almost entirely orange, with green between the veins, splashed with red; juvenile leaves deep green with an orange tinge.

C. v.p. **'Sanderi'**. A lobed leaf of bright green, with centre marking of yellow, later turning to orange, young stems red.

C. v.p. **'Secretaire Chevalliere'**. The blackish green leaves are veined and overlaid yellow, orange, and red.

C. v.p. **'Spirale'***. Long narrow green leaves with a yellow centre vein, twisted and spiralled like a corkscrew.

C. v.p. **'Stoplight'**. The green to blackish-green leaves are variegated yellow and red, juvenile leaves are cream flushed green.

C. v.p. **'Sunrise'**. Narrow green leaves veined and edged in red and orange; juvenile leaves veined and edged in yellow.

C. v.p. **'Suva'***. Slightly lobed, bright-green leaves occasionally veined and marked with yellow, orange and red.

Codiaeum (Croton) variegatum pictum 'Rising Sun'

Codiaeum (Croton) variegatum pictum 'Stoplight'

Codiaeum (Croton) variegatum pictum 'Sunrise'

Codiaeum (Croton) variegatum pictum 'Sanderi'

Codiaeum (Croton) variegatum pictum 'Secretaire Chevalliere'

C. v.p. **'Tartan'.** The long straight green-to-black leaves are heavily veined with yellow through orange to red.

C. v.p. **'Thai hybrids'.** These interesting dwarf Crotons have their twisted green to black leaves heavily variegated with yellow, orange, pink, and red.

C. v.p. **'The Queen'.** Large broad fresh-green leaves heavily marked in cream and yellow.

C. v.p. **'Undulatum'.** Large wavy-edged bronze and green leaves specked with red; contrasting pale green vein-pattern shows on the bronze underside.

C. v.p. **'Van Houtte'.** The green, red, and black leaves are variegated and veined with cream, orange, and red.

C. v.p. **'William Manning'*.** Large, almost yellow, leaves, green between the veins, orange-red beneath; juvenile leaves green, splashed with yellow.

Codiaeum (Croton) variegatum pictum 'Undulatum'

Codiaeum (Croton) variegatum pictum 'The Queen'

Codiaeum (Croton) variegatum pictum 'Thai hybrids'

Codiaeum (Croton) variegatum pictum 'Tartan'

Codiaeum (Croton) variegatum pictum 'Van Houtte' with 'Magnolaefolia'

COLEUS   Labiatae

Painted Nettle

The high colour of these rapid-growing plants provides brightness in the sheltered sections of the garden, plus useful pot plants for patios, bush-houses, sunrooms, and bright windows in the home.

Grow: In warm, frost-free, sheltered gardens, in filtered to bright sun.
Position indoors: Bright sunrooms or sunny windows.
Water: Keep moist, as these are thirsty plants.
Soil: Indoor Potting Mix.
Fertiliser: Complete Plant Food monthly, with foliar (Aquasol) between feedings, and during rapid growth.
Propagation: From seeds or preferred plants by cutting.
Pests and problems: Aphis and caterpillars. To keep short and bushy, regularly pinch back new shoots and remove flower spikes.

Varieties include:
C. amboinicus*. 3 in 1 Herb. Has thick, fleshy, very succulent, light-green leaves, which are strongly fragrant. A valuable kitchen herb, with a pleasant flavour. Of trailing habit.
C. blumei* (Java). Soft-stemmed plants producing beautifully marked leaves variegated in reds, yellows, whites, greens, and orange; the leaves may be toothed or heavily serrated; racemes of lilac flowers are produced during the summer months. Plants may be propagated from seed, but the choicer varieties are produced from cuttings and sold as plants.
C. b. **Broadleafed strain.** A broad-leafed strain of rather restricted colourings, mainly yellows, deep reds, fawn, orange, pink, etc., not so vividly variegated as the Rainbow Collection. They are, however, really exotic, with the broad fluted leaves heavily quilted.
C. b. **Rainbow strain.** A plain-leafed strain comprising a wide range of shades and variegations in the most brilliant colourings.
C. b. **Ruffled Exhibition strain***. This beautiful strain consists mainly of deep reds, orange, and pink which are heavily veined, some variegated and some marked black, and all heavily serrated and ruffled with green edgings.

Coleus Broad leafed strain

Coleus 'Rainbow' strain

106

COLUMNEA   Gesneriaceae

Columneas are bright, eye-catching, hanging pot plants which flower intermittently from spring to late autumn.

Grow: In glasshouses or warm bush-houses.
Position indoors: Ideal in hanging pots and macrame hangers, in sunrooms and near bright windows.
Water: Keep moist. Preferably immerse weekly.
Soil: Indoor Potting Mix.
Fertiliser: Complete Plant Food (dry, liquid, or foliar) monthly.
Propagation: From cuttings.
Pests and problems: None in particular.

Varieties include:
C. banksii. A basket trailer, with pendulous stems, along which are borne red flowers with yellow throat.
C. 'Campus Queen'. A stiffer growing variety, bearing orange flowers marked yellow.
C. 'Early Bird'. Has hanging reddish stems, deep green leaves, and yellow flowers, tipped with orange.
C. gloriosa (Costa Rica). A basket trailer, with pendulous stems, bearing small hairy oblong leaves, and solitary, horizontal growing, fiery-red, trumpet flowers, with yellow throats.
C. 'Goldrush'. Has hanging stems, and deep green leaves, which are purple beneath, flowers are canary-yellow.
*C. kewensis.** Has deep green shiny leaves, on trailing stems, and hairy orange red flowers.
C. kewensis 'Variegata'. As above with beautifully marked leaves, pink and white on glossy deep green.
C. microphylla (Costa Rica). Hangs down on long trailers, with small mid-green, hairy leaves; attractive red and yellow, tongue-like flowers.
C. 'Red Spear'. The green leaves are purple beneath, flowers are red veined yellow.
C. 'Yellow Dragon'. Has mid-green leaves on hanging stems, and yellow flowers.

Columnea microphylla   *Columnea 'Campus Queen'*

Columnea gloriosa   *Columnea banksii*

Columnea 'Early Bird'

Columnea 'Yellow Dragon'   *Columnea 'Red Spear'*

Columnea 'Goldrush'

Columnea kewensis 'Variegata'

CORDYLINE   Liliaceae

Ti Plant

Cordylines are often wrongly called red Dracaenas. Their impact of colour is welcomed in the tropical or warm, sheltered garden, or in pot plants for poolsides, patios, airy sunrooms or sunny, airy windows.

Grow: In sheltered gardens, bush-houses and glasshouses.
Position indoors: Use indoors in bright or sunny, airy positions for short periods, before rotating outdoors again.
Water: Keep moist.
Soil: General Potting Mix.
Fertiliser: Complete Plant Food monthly, or alternate with foliar (Aquasol).
Propagation: From end-cutting or 10-15 cm stem sections.
Pests and problems: Aphis, mites, and all chewing insects.

Varieties include:
C. terminalis (Malaya). Leaves coppery-green, shading to red; winter growth bright red; panicles of lilac flowers.
C. terminalis **'Alba Rosea'**. Brown-green leaves, heavily flushed with cream and red.
C. terminalis **'Amabilis'**. Nice, compact variety with leaves of deep green, flushed red. New growth blotched cream and red.
C. terminalis **'Angusta'** (Java). Long narrow coppery-green leaves, turning red.
C. terminalis **'Baby Doll'**. A dwarf variety, freely suckering at the base; becomes very colourful, in shades of clear red and pink, with red border (seedling strain).
C. terminalis **'Baby Doll'** or **'Dolly'**. A short thick variety, freely suckering at the base. Bronzy-red foliage, edged red and with brilliant red centre. Short and compact growth.
C. terminalis **'Baby Ti'** (Hawaii). Narrower variety, bronze-red edged red and brilliant red centre.
C. terminalis **'Bellulu'**. Upright, narrow, coppery-green leaves with bright-red edging, some leaves being mostly red.

Cordyline terminalis 'Angusta'

Cordyline terminalis 'Alba Rosea'

Cordyline terminalis 'Amabilis'

Cordyline terminalis 'Dolly' or 'Bab[y] Doll'

Cordyline terminalis

Cordyline terminalis 'Baby Doll' (seed strain)

Cordyline terminalis 'Baby Ti'

Cordyline terminalis 'Bellulu'

C. **terminalis** **'Bicolour'.** Broad metallic-green leaves edged and marked with red, and occasionally cream.

C. **terminalis** **'Inscripta'.** Narrow, twisting green leaves, bordered with red.

C. **terminalis** **'Margaret Storey'.** Bold large leaves of metallic red and green, with red edging.

C. **terminalis** **'Metallica'.** Broad, oval leaves of metallic coppery-red.

C. **terminalis** **'Pulchella'.** Narrow fresh-green leaves, surrounded with cream, red edging.

Cordyline terminalis 'Bicolour'

Cordyline terminalis 'Pulchella'

Cordyline terminalis 'Inscripta'

Cordyline terminalis 'Margaret Storey'

Cordyline terminalis 'Metallica'

CORDYLINE, continued

C. terminalis **'Rosea'.** Broad coppery-red leaves, edged with bright red.

C. terminalis **'Rubra'.** Broad leaves of greenish coppery-red with a narrow red edging.

C. terminalis **'Shot Silk'.** The green leaves are irregularly striped and flecked with cream, pink, and red.

C. terminalis **'Tricolour'.** The fresh green leaves are banded in pale green and cream, and edged in pink and red.

CYCAS   Cycadaceae

Sago Palm

These stiff palm-like plants are very slow-growing and may be planted in sheltered, dry corners of the garden or grown as pot plants on patios and even indoors.

Grow: In filtered sun, in garden or bush-house.
Position indoors: Sunroom, patio, or airy bright window.
Water: Keep on dry side and allow to dry out between waterings.
Soil: General Potting Mix.
Fertiliser: Complete Plant Food (dry, liquid, or foliar) every few months.
Propagation: From seeds.
Pests and problems: Few observed.

Varieties include:
C. revoluta (S. Japan to Java). Grows on trunk to 2–3 m high.
C. media* (N. Australia). The Australian Nut Palm. Trunk to 5 m high.

Cordyline terminalis 'Shot Silk'

Cordyline terminalis 'Rubra'   *Cordyline terminalis* 'Tricolour'

Cycas revoluta, Sago Palm

Cordyline terminalis 'Rosea'

CYCLAMEN   Primulaceae
Alpine Violet

Very popular flowering pot plants, grown the world over for indoor decoration. However, because of incorrect indoor positioning, many are lost prematurely.

Grow: In cool glasshouse or summer bush-house.

Position indoors: It is important to select an airy, bright window position indoors, or in a sunroom. If preferred, rotate plants from a sheltered verandah (filtered sun to bright light) on a weekly basis.

Water: Keep moist, preferably water by immersing. Empty saucers of excess water.

Soil: Indoor Potting Mix.

Fertiliser: Complete Plant Food every 2 months, and foliar feed every 2–3 weeks.

Propagation: From seeds or corms.

Pests and problems: Mites and caterpillars. Cyclamen are rarely as good for the second season. They are usually discarded and fresh ones grown. However, if you wish to try and keep them for a second season, lay the pots on their sides in a bush-house, or plunge them in the soil in a sheltered section of the garden. If they survive they should re-shoot the following autumn, when they may then be repotted.

Varieties include:

*C. persicum.** (Greece). A popular winter-flowering house plant for cool situations. Succulent heart-shaped bluish-green leaves with a silver design; upright flowers in reds, pinks, and mauves to white.

C. persicum giganteum. The usual florist's strain sold.

C. persicum 'Rococo'. The fringed edge strain. There are also dwarf strains.

DICHORISANDRA and CAMPELIA   Commelinaceae
Spiderwort

These colourful plants, associated with the 'Wandering Jews', are adaptable to indoor display, or terrarium use.

Grow: In warm glasshouses or summer bush-houses. Filtered sun.

Position indoors: Sunroom or near bright window, or terrarium (with grow-light).

Water: Keep evenly moist.

Soil: General Potting Mix.

Fertiliser: Complete Plant Food (dry, liquid, or foliar).

Propagation: From cutting. Replant the cut-back pieces for massed pots.

Pests and problems: Cut back regularly to keep compact. Take outdoors when lanky or unattractive.

Varieties include:

CAMPELIA
Variegated Dichorisandra

C. zanonia (A cultivar from Central America) Mexican Flag. A very colourful plant of the Dichorisandra species, with leaves of cream and green, edged red and flushed pink and purple.

DICHORISANDRA
Spiderwort

D. reginae (Peru). A slow-growing, upright plant with dark-green leaves, banded in silver, the centre metallic purplish-red; flowers lavender.

D. thysiflora (Brazil). Blue Ginger. A cane-stemmed plant with narrow green leaves and an attractive head of deep-blue flowers with yellow centres.

Cyclamen persicum 'Rococo', Ruffled Alpine Violet

Dichorisandra reginae, Queen's Spiderwort

Dichorisandra thysiflora, Blue Ginger

Campelia zanonia, Mexican Flag

DIEFFENBACHIA   Araceae

Dumb Canes

Dumb Canes are so named because it is said that the sap will swell the tongue and make speech difficult. Hence the name 'Mother-in-Law Plant' has also gained popularity. Dieffenbachias are one of the more successful indoor plants where temperatures above 16°C can be maintained during winter. During summer temperatures they thrive in all areas. With the recent introduction of the newer varieties, 'Tropic Snow', and the clustering varieties of 'Exotica Perfection', 'Camille', and 'Galaxy', Dieffenbachia have become even more popular.

Grow: In glasshouses, or similar, above 16°C–18°C.
Position indoors: Warm sunroom or indoors near bright, warm window.
Water: Water thoroughly and allow to dry between waterings.
Soil: General Potting Mix.
Fertiliser: Complete Plant Food monthly.
Propagation: From cuttings or division of clustered plants.
Pests and problems: Spider mites. Avoid winter chills from being too close to the window glass.

Varieties include:
D. amoena (Colombia, Costa Rica). Thick stemmed variety, with large green leaves evenly marked in cream. Very durable indoors.
***D. amoena* 'Tropic Snow'** ('Snow Queen'). Similar with heavier cream markings.
D. × bausei (Brazil). Yellowish-green leaf with deep-green and white spots and deep-green edging.
D. 'Camille'. Handsome new introduction, cream leaf with green edging. Clustering nicely. 'Marianne' is similar in colouring and height.
D. chelsonii (Colombia). Deep-green leaf, with a silver-grey centre in a feather design.
D. 'Exotica' (Costa Rica). A beautifully marked variety with green oval-pointed leaves liberally sprinkled with ivory-cream.
D. 'Exotica Perfection'. Similar to above, but forms a dense cluster of stems, good indoors. New introduction.
D. 'Galaxy' ('Welkerii'). Bright highly coloured new introduction to the clustering range.
D. 'Marianne'. Similarly marked with creamy white leaves edged in green, clustering.

Dieffenbachia 'Marianne'

Dieffenbachia amoena

Dieffenbachia × *bausei*

Dieffenbachia 'Exotica Perfection'

Dieffenbachia 'Exotica'

Dieffenbachia 'Camille'

Dieffenbachia 'Galaxy'

Dieffenbachia 'Golden Treasure'

Dieffenbachia amoena 'Tropic Snow'
('Snow Queen' or 'Hi-colour')

112

Dieffenbachia hoffmannii

Dieffenbachia maculata 'Rudolph Roehrs'

D. hoffmannii (Costa Rica). An attractive satiny dark-green leaf, spotted in white and with a white midrib.

D. leopoldii* (Costa Rica). This variety has velvety deep emerald-green leaves with a contrasting white midrib.

D. maculata* (picta) (Brazil). The original species with the bright green leaves spotted and blotched in cream.

D. maculata jenmannii (Guiana). Long, oblong, fresh-green leaves with ivory cross-band design.

D. maculata 'Rudolph Roehrs'. A very striking variety with leaves which are mostly yellow, spotted in ivory and ribbed and edged with deep green.

D. maculata 'Superba'. This very striking variety has fresh-green leaves, heavily variegated with creamy-white.

D. × memoria corsii*. Greyish leaf with large green blotches and occasional ivory spots.

D. sequina decora (Brazil). The deep green leaves are marked in white and silver, with creamy spots.

D. sequina irrorata (Brazil). Oblong-pointed, thinly textured, yellow leaves, with dark-green edging and blotching, stem whitish.

D. sequina lineata* (Venezuela, Colombia). A robust species with deep-green long oblong leaves and white-striped stems.

D. × splendens. Black-green leaf with white centre vein and greenish and creamy spots.

Dieffenbachia sequina decora

Dieffenbachia maculata 'Superba'

Dieffenbachia sequina irrorata

Dieffenbachia × splendens

Dieffenbachia maculata jenmannii   113

DORSTENIA
Moraceae

Mattress Button Plant

A small plant with large glossy deep-green leaves and curious rubber-like flowers. Resembles a mattress button. They are close relatives of the Rubber Plant family. Previously called Elastostemmon.

Grow: In glasshouses.
Position indoors: Sunroom or near a window. Also good in terrariums.
Water: Keep moist.
Soil: General Potting Mix.
Fertiliser: Complete Plant Food every 1–2 months.
Propagation: From seed or division. Once a plant is obtained, I have observed them popping up in other pot plants and in ground areas around them.
Pests and problems: None observed.

Varieties include:
D. turneraefolia (Trop. America). A small plant with large glossy deep-green leaves and curious rubber-like flowers. Good indoors.

Dorstenia turneraefolia, Mattress Button Plant

DRACAENA
Liliaceae

Happy Plants or Dragon Plants

These hardy plants are widely used indoors as well as outdoors in temperate and tropical regions, and are known as Dragon Plants. When the shooting stem cuts are grown in water and attractively displayed for sale in small fancy pots they are known as Happy Plants. They are very popular in this latter form, and may later be transferred to soil and grown as other Dracaenas.

Grow: In sheltered garden areas or in pots on patios and poolsides. Start in glasshouses or warm bush-houses.
Position indoors: In sunroom or near natural light. Will tolerate poor light for short periods.
Water: Keep moist.
Soil: General Potting Mix.
Fertiliser: Complete Plant Food monthly, alternating with foliar.
Propagation: From cuttings. Happy Plants are grown by cutting thick trunk sections into lengths of 10-15 cm, branched sections longer, and standing upright in attractive containers. Fill in with marble chips or something similar, and keep filled with clean water. They soon shoot away.
Pests and problems: Few observed. Variegated varieties require stronger sun to retain colour.

Varieties include:

DRACAENA

D. cannaefolia*. Appears to be a green *sanderiana* species, growing on slender upright canes, with deep-green lanceolate leaves. Very durable.
D. deremensis **'Janet Craig'**. Glossy broad green leaves.
D. deremensis **'Longii'** (Africa). Glossy deep-green leaf with a broad clear white centre stripe.
D. deremensis **'Warneckii'** (Africa). Fresh-green leaf with milky-green centre banded by a white stripe either side, leaving a bright-green edging.
D. deremensis **'Bausei'***. Similar but with the white bands closer together toward the centre.
D. fragrans (West Africa). Broad glossy green leaves.
D. fragrans **'Lindenii'** (Africa). Greenish to yellow leaves edged and centre-striped with deep green.

An arrangement of Dracaena 'cuts' growing in water as 'Happy Plants'

Dracaena deremensis 'Janet Craig'

Dracaena fragrans

Dracaena fragrans 'Lindenii'

Dracaena deremensis 'Longii'

Dracaena deremensis 'Warneckii', Striped Dracaena

115

DRACAENA, etc., continued

***D. fragrans* 'Massangeana'** (Africa). Deep-green leaf with a broad centre band of light green to yellow.

***D. fragrans* 'Victoriae'*.** The cream to yellow leaves have a centre band of green streaked silver grey.

D. godseffiana (Africa). A small shrubby plant with small dark-green oval leaves, spotted in yellow and borne on thin, wiry stems.

***D. godseffiana* 'Florida Beauty'.** Similar to the species, with heavier variegation; very striking.

***D. godseffiana* 'Milky Way'.** A striking variety, similar to the specie, with the deep green leaves spotted creamy yellow, and also having a broad centre band.

D. goldieana (Guinea). Queen of Dracaenas. A spectacular variety, requiring high humidity, with ovate glossy deep-green leaves on stalks, marked with cross-bands of pale green to white.

Dracaena fragrans 'Massangeana', Cornstalk Plant

Dracaena godseffiana 'Milky Way' (syn. 'Friedman')

Dracaena godseffiana, 'Florida Beauty'

Dracaena goldieana, Queen of Dracaenas

Dracaena godseffiana, Gold-dust Dracaena

Dracaena marginata, Madagascar Dragon Tree

D. marginata (Madagascar). Narrow deep-green leaves, edged with red.

***D. marginata* 'Tricolour'.** The beautiful variegated form, flushed with red.

D. sanderiana (Africa). Narrow twisted leaves, deep green and broad white edging. Erect on slender cane.

D. sanderiana virescens (Congo). The green leaves have a paler green centre stripe. Thin wavy stems. (Illus. p. 118.)

D. surculosa punculata (Sierra Leone). Branching variety resembling *godseffiana* but spotting is paler and in some cases green. Used a lot indoors.

Dracaena marginata 'Tricolour', Rainbow Tree

Dracaena sanderiana, Ribbon Plant

Dracaena surculosa punculata

117

DRACAENA, etc., continued

PLEOMELE

These have been renamed Dracaenas, and so have been included in this section. Their care is the same as Dracaenas, except that they prefer a little more winter warmth.

P. angustifolia honoriae (Solomon Islands, Torres Strait Islands). The green leaves are narrowly banded in creamy-yellow. Tall lanky trunks.

P. reflexa **'Variegata'** (S. India, Sri Lanka). Song of India. The leaves are beautifully variegated in creamy yellow. Thin wavy stems.

Dracaena sanderiana virescens

Pleomele angustifolia honoriae

Pleomele reflexa 'Variegata', Song of India

EPIPREMNUM and SCINDAPSUS
Araceae

Pothos

Some Pothos varieties have been renamed *Epipremnum* and *Scindapsus*. Along with their relatives, Philodendrons, they are hardy indoor creepers. They are best grown on totems, so that their leaves will improve in size and apperarance. Cut lengths may also be grown in water.

Grow: Best grown in warm glasshouses. However, in the tropics and subtropics these may be grown up the trunks of trees, where the leaves will grow to almost 1 m in length.
Position indoors: Near bright window or diffused sunlight, or in a sunroom.
Water: Soil may dry out between waterings. If on totems, keep these moist.
Soil: Indoor Potting Mix.
Fertiliser: Complete Plant Food, monthly during summer or foliar fertiliser to foliage every 2–3 weeks.
Propagation: From cuttings. Always select the best coloured cuttings.
Pests and problems: General observation.

Varieties include:

EPIPREMNUM

E. aureus (Solomon Islands). Devil's Ivy. Trailer, with glossy green leaves splashed with yellow variegation.
E. aureus **'All Gold'**. New. The leaf pure gold if kept in good light.
E. aureus **'Marble Queen'**. Similar to *aureus*, but the green leavers are variegated with white. Keep this variety warmer and drier. Regularly cut out the all green sections of the plant to hold the colourful variegation.
E. pinnatum (Malaya, E. Indies, New Guinea). Taro Vine. The green leaves segment as they grow larger.

SCINDAPSUS

S. pictus argyraeus (Borneo). Satin Pothos. In this trailer, the bluish-green leaves are spotted with silver. The leaves are usually small, but will grow larger if the plant is attached to a totem.

Epipremnum (Scindapsus) pictus argyraeus, Satin Pothos

Epipremnum (Pothos) aureus 'All Gold'

Epipremnum (Pothos) aureus 'Marble Queen'

Epipremnum pinnatum, Taro Vine

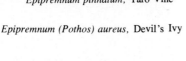

Epipremnum (Pothos) aureus, Devil's Ivy

EPISCIA   Gesneriaceae

Flame Violets

These colourful relatives of Aeschynanthus, Columneas, and Saintpaulias prefer hanging pots or baskets. They require temperatures above 20°C to make growth.

Grow: In heated (winter) glasshouses.

Position indoors: Warm sunroom, hanging above other plants, for added humidity, or similar bright window position indoors. Also good in a lit terrarium.

Water: Keep evenly moist.

Soil: Indoor Potting Mix.

Fertiliser: Complete Plant Food monthly during growth period or alternate with foliar (Aquasol).

Propagation: From cuttings, or small hanging plantlets.

Pests and problems: Observe for spider mites.

Varieties include:

E. cupreata **'Frosty'** (Colombia). Chocolate Soldiers. The puckered coppery-green leaves are marked silver. Red flowers.

E. cupreata **'Silver Sheen'.** Of similar habit to the above, but with bright-green leaves having a margin of silver.

E. dianthiflora* (Mexico). This freely hanging variety has green leaves and nicely fringed white flowers.

E. lilacina (Costa Rica). Blue-flowered Teddy Bear. Has silver-veined leaves and larger lilac-blue flowers, which only last 3–4 days.

E. punctata (Guatemala). Similar to *Dianthiflora*, but with purple spots.

E. reptans (Northern S. America). The brownish-green leaves are vividly veined silver. Red flowers.

Episcia cupreata 'Frosty', Flame Violet

Episcia cupreata 'Silver Sheen', Flame Violet

Episcia lilacina, Blue Flowered Teddy Bear

Episcia punctata, Spotted Lace Flower Vine

120   *Episcia reptans*, Flame Violet

EUCHARIS　　　Amaryllidaceae

Eucharis Lily

E. grandiflora (Amazon). This bulb is a popular pot plant in ferneries, particularly in Queensland. The foliage resembles an *Aspidistra,* and the flower is similar to a white daffodil. It requires a warm location, such as a glasshouse, and may be taken indoors for its flowering period. Water as required to keep moist. Put into General Potting Mix. Continue to fertilise with Complete Plant Food monthly, after flowering.

EUPHORBIA　　　Euphorbiaceae

Poinsettia

No indoor display seems complete without a pot of Poinsettia. Given good light, these plants flower for many months, indoors. They may then be planted in a warm corner of the garden, or kept on as an indoor foliage plant.

Grow: As pot plants, they are grown in glasshouses under specially controlled light and dark conditions, to prematurely flower at given times of the year. They may also be grown to flower normally in winter, without this extra treatment.

Position indoors: Sunroom or bright, sunny window.

Water: Allow to dry between waterings.

Soil: General Potting Mix.

Fertiliser: Complete Plant Food (dry, liquid, or foliar) every month, to prevent leaves from yellowing and falling.

Propagation: From cuttings.

Pests and problems: None observed.

Varieties include:

E. pulcherrima (Southern Mexico). Poinsettia. Branching shrub, winter deciduous, with large flower bracts in colours of red, pink, creamy pink, and creamy white. These are the main ones grown for indoor culture, but numerous others are also widely grown outdoors, including the double 'Henrietta Ecke'.

Eucharis grandiflora, Eucharis Lily or Amazon Lily

Euphorbia pulcherrima 'Ecke's White', Cream Poinsettia

Euphorbia pulcherrima 'Annette Hegg', Red Poinsettia

Euphorbia pulcherrima 'Rosea', Pink Poinsettia

EUPHORBIA, continued

E. splendens* (Madagascar). Crown of Thorns. Brownish stem covered with thorns and occasional dull green leaves; small scarlet flowers.

E. tirucalli (Uganda, Congo, Zanzibar). Milk Bush. Also called 'Naked Lady'. Cylindrical pencil-thick branches, with poisonous milk, and narrow deciduous leaves.

Euphorbia tirucalli, Milk Bush or Naked Lady

PEDILANTHUS
Zigzag Plant

These erect-growing, deciduous Euphorbias may be found in most tropical collections. As an indoor pot plan' they are hardy, and usually retain most of their foliage during winter, when the variegated forms have become suffused with pink.

Grow: Outdoors in tropics and subtropics and in warm summer bush-house or glasshouse in temperate areas.

Varieties include:

P. smallii (Brazil). The branching stems have deep-green leaves, which are heavily variegated with cream, later pink.

P. tithymaloides (America). An upright-growing plant on tall, slender blackish-green stems, with small, deep-green, zigzag, opposite-growing leaves; red flowers.

P. tithymaloides '**Variegatus**' (W. Indies). Similar in growth to the above, with pale green leaves, highly variegated with white and tinged red.

Pedilanthus tithymaloides – showing flowers

Pedilanthus smallii

Pedilanthus tithymaloides 'Variegatus', Zig Zag Plant

SYNADENIUM
Milk Bush

S. grantii (E. Africa). Has yellow-green leaves, with deeper green veins, on thick, succulent branches. Red flowers. Care as above.

Synadenium grantii, Milk Bush

FERNS

Ferns are probably the most popular of indoor plants. There are so many beautiful species from which to choose, and their lush greenery will enhance any room. Unfortunately, many beautiful ferns die each year, the owners not realising that the average soft, lush fern requires 50% humidity or more to survive. One way to provide this is to plant ferns in a terrarium; another is to mist the foliage a few times a day; or grow them in a sunroom which contains a number of other plants; or by placing a plastic bag or bell-jar over the plants to retain the humidity; or by standing the pot on a large saucer of always-damp pebbles. These, however, are tedious procedures, and it would be better to select only the hardier ferns which will tolerate less than 50% humidity. These include *Adiantum hispidum* (Australian Maidenhair), *Asplenium* (Bird's Nest), *Cyrtomium* (Holly Fern), *Nephrolepis* (Boston types), *Pellae rotundifolia* (Button Ferns), and *Platycerium* (Elkhorn). You could also try any other ferns with a tougher type of foliage. To maintain your ferns indoors, I offer the following hints:

Light: Keep them out of direct, hot sun. Early morning sun is all right, but keep them in good light.
Humidity: Place your ferns on large saucers filled with pebbles to the top of the rim, and keep this moist. Mist the foliage down as many times as is convenient.
Water: Keep your ferns moist, not over-wet, as the tiny roots can be damaged by too much moisture.
Soil: Indoor Potting Mix is all right if it contains peat moss. If not, add up to 25% of peat moss.
Fertiliser: Many complete ones are suitable, but use in the soil sparingly. Foliar (Aquasol or similar) at half strength fortnightly, over the foliage is also good.
Propagation: May be from spores, division, or even plantlets which appear on the leaves of some varieties.
Pests and problems: Watch for aphis, scale, or mealy bug.

ADIANTUM
Maidenhair Fern
Polypodiaceae

The dainty Maidenhair Ferns are always popular favourites. A few are hardy enough for the garden, but generally the prettier the variety, the more tender it is, and would be best grown in fernery or glasshouse conditions.

Special notes:
* Do not over-water.
* Move outside at first signs of distress.
* Remember Maidenhair ferns have a rest period. They may be divided and repotted at that time, after the old, dying leaves have been removed.

Varieties include:
A. charlottae parvifolium. Very fine variety.
A. davisii multiceps. Medium-fine and very thick.
A. 'Farleyensis' (Barbados). Beautiful medium-sized, new growth is pink.

Adiantum charlottae parvifolium, Fine Maidenhair

Adiantum davisii multiceps

Adiantum 'Farleyensis', Barbados Maidenhair

123

FERNS, continued

A. **hispidulum** (Australia). Australian Maidenhair. Stiff, robust growth. Hardy.
A. **microphyllum** (Afghanistan, India). Very fine variety.
A. **trapeziforme** (Central America). Giant Maidenhair. Large-leafed variety.
A. **'Valley Mist'** (Tasmania). Medium-sized, hardy for outdoor use; quick recovery from indoor abuse.
A. **'Weigandii'.** Medium-sized and very thick.

Adiantum trapeziforme, Giant Maidenhair

Adiantum 'Weigandii'

Adiantum 'Valley Mist'

Adiantum hispidulum, Australian Maidenhair

Adiantum microphyllum, Fine Maidenhair Fern

ASPLENIUM
Bird's Nest Fern
Polypodiaceae

These tough native Australian ferns are very popular for ferneries or sheltered garden corners. They may also be used as indoor pot plants or terrarium subjects.

Varieties include:
A. bulbiferum (Australia, New Zealand, Malaysia). Hen and Chicken Fern or Mother Fern, so called because it is frequently seen with its young ferns growing above the leaves from spores. The young fernlets of *bulbiferum* may be removed when large enough, and planted in a mix rich in peat moss, or sphagnum moss, then grown on tall, larger plants and then potted. They take about 2 years to mature.
A. nidus (Asia to Queensland). Bird's Nest or Crow's Nest Fern. Handsome, shiny rosette of broad leaves. Frequently used indoors, or even in the filtered light of an open garden.

BLECHNUM
Rib Fern
Polypodiaceae

These attractive palm-like ferns are suitable as pot plants in warmer areas. A minimum evening temperature of 16°C is needed. They prefer the humus soil slightly more alkaline. Add lime or dolomite.

Varieties include:
B. brasiliense (Brazil, Peru). Has broad, wavy leaves. Juvenile foliage is bronzy. Grows to 1 m.
B. gibbum (New Caledonia). Has narrower leaves and grows to 1.5 m.

Blechnum gibbum, Rib Fern

Asplenium nidus, Bird's Nest or Crow's Nest

Blechnum brasiliense, Rib Fern

Top left: *Polystichum setiferum proliferum*. Right: *Pteris quadriaurita* 'Argyraea'. Bottom left: *Asplenium bulbiferum*, Hen and Chicken or Mother Fern

125

CYRTOMIUM   Polypodiaceae
Holly Fern

C. falcatum **'Rochfortianum'**. (India, Japan, China, Hawaii). A widely grown cultivar fern, which is quite hardy indoors. It has broader fronds than *falcatum*. It prefers cooler temperatures and no sun.

Cyrtomium falcatum 'Rochfortianum', Holly Fern

DAVALLIA   Polypodiaceae
Hare's Foot Fern

Davallias are widely used as indoor plants, where they are reasonably successful, if kept in temperatures of above 16°C. Prefer good light, with high humidity. For best results, the running rhizomes prefer to be over the edge of a fern basket or better still a hollowed-out block of tree-fern trunk.

Varieties include:
D. fejeensis (Fiji). A fine fern with brown hair-covered rhizomes, which trail over the edges of pots.
d. fejeensis **'Plumosa'**. A very fine form, with plume-like fronds.

Davallia fejeensis, Rabbit's Foot or Hare's Foot Fern

Davallia fejeensis 'Plumosa', Fine Hare's Foot Fern

DORYOPTERIS   Polypodiaceae
Hand Fern

D. palmata (W. Indies, Peru, Brazil). A small fern with unusual, fingered leaves, of shiny, deep green. It requires temperatures with a minimum of 16°C, filtered light to no sun, and high humidity.

Doryopteris palmata, Hand Fern

LYCOPODIUM   Lycopodiaceae
Queensland Tassel Fern

L. phlegmaria (Queensland). This popular rope-like, hanging fern is pale green. Usually grown in ferneries in warmer climates or glasshouses in cooler climates. It is propagated by cuttings or spores.

Lycopodium phlegmaria, Queensland Tassel Fern

LYGODIUM
Japanese Climbing Fern
Schizaeaceae

L. japonicum (Japan to India, E. Indies, northern Australia). Has fine twining stems with fresh green leaves. Very dainty creeper for macrame hanger, in a brightly lit room, or sunroom. Prefers humidity and will tolerate cool temperatures to 10°C. Keep evenly moist.

Varieties include:
N. biserrata furcans (Central America, Africa, Hong Kong, Queensland). Fishtail Fern. Grows long fronds, with toothed edges.
N. cordifolia **'Duffii'** (New Zealand, Polynesia). A smaller variety, with narrow, erect fronds of small, roundish leaves.
N. cordifolia **'Plumosa'** (Japan to New Zealand). Has narrower, plain leaves which later broaden and become lacey on the edges.

Lygodium japonicum, Japanese Climbing Fern

Nephrolepis biserrata furcans, Fishtail Fern

Nephrolepis cordifolia 'Duffii', Pigmy Sword Fern

NEPHROLEPIS
Boston Fern, Lace Fern
Polypodiaceae

Nephrolepis would be the most popular ferns grown for market to-day. Many of the varieties are quite successful indoors and 'Kimberley Queen' *(obliterata)* has been chosen 'House Plant for 1982'. While all varieties have some success indoors, the coarser varieties such as *bostoniensis* should give pleasure for longer periods, under harder conditions. If grown in a sunroom or brightly lit and airy indoor position, close to a light source, the 'Bostons' and more vigorous varieties will grow quite lengthy 'trails', which in turn grow pendulous plantlets, making a very showy plant. These may be removed when large enough, during warm conditions, and potted. Larger pots may also be divided and re-potted during warmer temperatures. Keep moist, preferably by immersing the entire pot, at least each 1–2 weeks, and topping-up in between.

Nephrolepis cordifolia 'Plumosa'

FERNS, continued

N. exaltata bostoniensis. Boston Fern. Larger growing and graceful with fronds to 1 m, and hanging trails to the ground.
N. exaltata bostoniensis compacta. Dwarf Boston Fern. More compact with numerous spreading fronds.
N. exaltata bostoniensis aurea **'Fan Dancer'.** A new release and a golden version of the above.
N. exaltata **'Childsii'.** A small clustering variety, with the short fronds curled and fully laced.
N. exaltata **'Elegantissima'.** A medium variety, with coarsely laced fronds, very sturdy.
N. exaltata **'Fluffy Ruffles'*.** A dwarf variety with upright fronds densely fluffy and turning under at the ends.
N. exaltata **'Hilli'.** A sturdy, large variety with the long and narrower fronds wavy and overlapping.

Nephrolepis exaltata bostoniensis, Boston Fern

Nephrolepis exaltata bostoniensis compacta, Dwarf Boston Fern

Nephrolepis exaltata 'Hillii'

Nephrolepis exaltata bostoniensis aurea, Fan Dancer Fern

Nephrolepis exaltata 'Elegantissima'

Nephrolepis exaltata 'Childsii'

Nephrolepis exaltata 'Whitmanii', Lace Fern

N. exaltata 'Muscosa'*. A dwarf and upright variety with the still, plain fronds becoming heavily laced.

N. exaltata 'Nuebertii'. Loose hanging fronds, coarse at first, but becoming lacy and fine as they mature.

N. exaltata 'Rooseveltii'. Widely grown commercially. The plain leaves become broad and stiffly laced.

N. exaltata 'Smithii'. A real lace-fern. The broad fronds, to 30 cm, are finely laced and overlapping. It is best watered by wetting the soil, rather than the foliage, to prevent rotting.

N. exaltata 'Suzy Wong'. A small variety with the broad leaves fine and thickly laced.

N. exaltata 'Verona'. Commercially grown. A nice fine variety, with the broad hanging fronds finely laced.

N. exaltata 'Whitmanii'. Medium-sized variety with the broad fronds becoming fine and thickly laced.

N. obliterata 'Kimberley Queen'. 'House Plant for 1982'. A medium-sized variety, resembling a Boston Fern, with stiffer angling fronds and hanging trails. Durable indoors.

Nephrolepis exaltata 'Rooseveltii', Stiff Lace Fern

Nephrolepis obliterata, Kimberley Queen

Nephrolepis exaltata 'Smithii', Fine Lace Fern

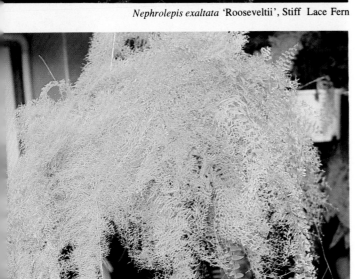

Nephrolepis exaltata 'Verona', Dwarf Lace Fern

Nephrolepis exaltata 'Nuebertii'

Nephrolepis exaltata 'Suzy Wong'

129

FERNS, continued

PELLAEA   Polypodiaceae
Button Fern

Varieties include:
P. rotundifolia (New Zealand). Button Fern. A low, spreading fern for pot or hanging basket and fairly adaptable for sunroom or indoor use. It likes humidity, prefers cool temperatures. Allow to dry between waterings. Shallow pots are best.
P. viridis (W. Indies). This bushy variety requires more warmth and humidity, and should be kept moist.

Varieties include:
*P. bifurcatum** (Eastern Australia). Elkhorn. Usually mounted on trees or boards. Plants multiply.
P. diversifolium. Erect Elkhorn. Widely used for pot-growing because of its erect habit of growth. Plants multiply.
P. grande (Eastern Australia to Philippines) Staghorn. Grows to a beautiful single plant. Reproduction is by growing spores.
P. hillii (Queensland). This differs from *bifurcatum* in the greater number of lobed ends to the fronds. Also grown as a pot plant. It is marketed as an Elkhorn in Queensland.

Pellae rotundifolia, Button Fern

Pellae viridis, Table Fern

Platycerium hillii, Queensland Elkhorn.

PLATYCERIUM   Polypodiaceae
Elkhorn, Staghorn

Platyceriums are widely marketed, either taken from trees in the bush, or sold as mounted plants ready for hanging. Occasionally they are sold as pot plants. While certain varieties are adaptable for pot-growing, most end up being mounted for wall-hanging or directly attached to trees. Unmounted plants can easily be attached to trees or boards, and many products can be used as a backing if the plant and the mount are of different shapes. You may use bagging, or a piece of carpet, or anything that will hold moisture. If nothing is required, a smearing of peatmoss will do the trick; the plant soon attaches if kept moist.

Platyceriums may be kept indoors, but should be taken outside once a week and thoroughly moistened with the hose. Liquid or foliar fertilisers are best, every 1–2 weeks at weaker strengths.

Platycerium grande, Staghorn

130

Platycerium diversifolium, Erect Elkhorn

POLYPODIUM   Polypodiaceae
Hare's Foot Fern

Varieties include:
P. angustifolium (Central America). Ribbon Fern. Ideal for hanging basket and adaptable indoors. Long strap-like, glossy leaves.
P. aureum **'Glaucophyllum'** (W. Indies). Hare's Foot Fern. Has blue-green leaves on golden, hairy feet.
P. formosanum. The Grub Fern. Fresh green leaves on grey rhizomes with roots, resembling a caterpillar walking from the pot.
P. punctatum **'Grandiceps'.** Fish Tail Fern. Clustering fern with crested tips. Grows indoors.
P. punctatum **'Serrulata'.** This fern has deeply serrated leaves which are most attractive.

Polypodium punctatum 'Serrulata'

Polypodium formosanum, Grub Fern

Polypodium aureum 'Glaucophyllum', Hare's Foot Fern

Polypodium angustifolium, Ribbon Fern

Polypodium punctatum 'Grandiceps', Fish Tail Fern

131

FERNS, continued

POLYSTICHUM   Polypodiaceae
Hedge Fern

Varieties include:
P. setiferum (all tropical and temperate zones). Hedge Fern. Glossy, green fronds set on brown, hairy stems. Tolerates cool conditions.
P. setiferum **'Proliferum'** (Australia). Filigree Fern. Similar to above but bears young plantlets along the fronds.

Polystichum setiferum, Hedge Fern

Polystichum setiferum 'Proliferum', Filigree Fern

PTERIS   Polypodiaceae
Table Fern, Brake Fern

Widely grown and marketed as commercial ferns, they are used indoors quite successfully.

Varieties include:
P. cretica **'Albo Lineata'.** Attractive creamy-white, variegated fern. Does well in low humidity. Keep moist but do not stand in water.
P. ensiformis **'Victoriae'.** Widely grown variety, with silvery-white variegation. Also used indoors.
P. quadriaurita **'Argyraea'.** (Central India). Silver Fern. Large fern to 1 m, bluish-green fronds, with silver-white centre.
P. tremula (New Zealand, eastern Australia). Australian Bracken. A prolific fern with short-lived bracts, which should be removed, and which are soon replaced.
P. umbrosa (New South Wales). A hardy variety with stiff, narrow, green leaves, which are shiny and attractive.

Pteris cretica 'Albo Lineata'

Pteris ensiformis 'Victoriae'

Pteris tremula, Australian Bracken

Pteris umbrosa

Pteris quadriaurita 'Argyraea'

SELAGINELLA
Selaginellaceae
Moss Fern

Varieties include:
S. cuspidata (Cuba, Central America). A most attractive fern with fresh, green fronds and upright growth. Best in a terrarium.
S. umbrosa (Central America). Erect stems of light green fronds to 30 cm.

Selaginella cuspidata, Moss Fern

Selaginella umbrosa, Moss Fern

FICUS
Moraceae
Figs or Rubber Trees

The Fig family. These hardy plants are very widely used both indoors and outdoors. They range from the hardy Rubber Plants to the leafy Weeping Fig and the variegated Creeping Fig. Some varieties are too vigorous for garden plantings, so are best retained in pots as long as possible, before transferring to large open areas.

Grow: Start in glasshouse, grow in warm bush-house or sheltered position outdoors. Suitable as pot plants on patios or verandahs.
Position indoors: The green rubber plants are hardy in most indoor positions, but prefer good light. The variegated rubber plants prefer bright, airy positions. *F. benjamina* and *F. hillii* are best conditioned to deep shade for a month before being taken indoors, as there is less defoliation. Then they require bright light, where they will regrow abundant foliage. The creeping *radicans* varieties will grow in hanging pots or on totems or ladders, and if used indoors require a brightly lit, airy position.
Water: Keep evenly moist, preferably immerse pots.
Soil: General Potting Mix.
Fertiliser: Complete Plant Food (dry, liquid, or foliar) monthly.
Propagation: Some from seed, all from cuttings.
Pests and problems: Few observed, very hardy.

Varieties include:
F. benjamina (India, Malaysia). Weeping Fig. Grows to a large tree with drooping branches of smallish green leaves. Prized indoors, where light is good. Good outdoor pot plant also.

Ficus benjamina, Weeping Fig

FICUS, continued

F. elastica* (India, Malaysia). Rubber Plant. Leathery, dark, glossy-green leaves on brown stems; young leaves enclosed in a rosy sheath.

F. elastica 'Burgundy'. Handsome deep, blackish-purple variant of *robusta*. Short-noded.

F. elastica 'Decora' (Indonesia). Deep-green leaves, broader and heavier than *F. elastica,* and the ivory midrib is red beneath.

F. elastica 'Doescheri'. A very striking form with green, grey, white and cream variegated foliage while the leaf veins and stems turn pink. Best outdoors.

F. elastica 'Robusta'. Similar to *decora,* but deeper colour and shorter noded.

F. elastica 'Schryveriana'. This heavily variegated form is very handsome. Best outdoors, unless light is good.

F. 'Green Island'. A new introduction, with thick, smallish, oval leaves. Compact and very branched. Green berries cover the stems.

Ficus elastica 'Burgundy', Burgundy Rubber Plant

Ficus elastica 'Decora', Wide Leaf Rubber Plant

Ficus elastica 'Doescheri', Variegated Rubber Plant

Ficus elastica 'Robusta', Rubber Plant

Ficus elastica 'Schryveriana'

Ficus 'Green Island', Dwarf Rubber Plant

F. longifolia. A new and handsome introduction, with longish leaves. Resembles a large leafed form of *benjamina*.

F. lyrata (pandurata) (Tropical W. Africa). Fiddleleaf Fig. This tree has large, leathery, fiddle-shaped, wavy deep-green leaves.

F. macrophylla (Australia). Moreton Bay Fig. Deep-green foliage somewhat resembling *elastica* in the juvenile stage, but having smaller leaves.

F. microphylla 'Hillii'. A handsome tree, resembling *benjamina*, with glossy rich green leaves. Same uses.

F. parcellii (South Pacific Islands). Clown Fig. A handsome variegated shrub, which bears fruits that are also variegated.

F. radicans 'Variegata'. (East Indies). A self-clinging trailer with smallish, pointed, rough, green leaves, variegated with creamy-white.

F. rubiginosa 'Variegata'* (Australia). A small tree, freely-branching, its deep green leaves marked with yellow and cream.

Ficus macrophylla, Moreton Bay Fig

Ficus longifolia

Ficus microphylla 'Hillii', Hill's Fig

Ficus parcellii, Clown Fig

Ficus radicans 'Variegata', Variegated Climbing Fig

Ficus lyrata (pandurata), Fiddle-leaf Fig

FILICIUM
Sapindaceae

Fern Tree

F. decipiens (India, Sri Lanka). This attractive, small tree has long, narrow, shiny, deep green leaves arranged in layers along the plant. It is quite good indoors, as well as growing outdoors in warm, sheltered positions.

Grow: In glasshouse or warm bush-house.
Position indoors: Sunroom or near bright window.
Water: Keep moist during growing period.
Soil: General Potting Mix.
Fertiliser: Complete Plant Food (dry, liquid, or foliar) monthly during growing period.
Propagation: From seed.
Pests and problems: Observe for mealy bug.

FITTONIA
Acanthaceae

Nerve Plant

Nerve Plants are warmth-loving plants, and will not retain their foliage under 17°C–19°C. At lower temperatures they will hold better in lighted terrariums. During warmer summer temperatures they can be grown in hanging pots, around the tops of pots containing more leggy plants, or in broad pots on their own.

Grow: In winter-heated glasshouses.
Position indoors: Warm sunroom or near warm window. Ideal in lighted terrarium.
Water: Keep moist during summer growth, less during winter growth.
Soil: General Potting Mix.
Fertiliser: Complete Plant Food every 2 months, foliar (Aquasol) every 2–3 weeks during growth period.
Propagation: From cuttings.
Pests and problems: Retain high humidity by occasionally hosing the foliage.

Varieties include:
F. verschaffeltii (Peru). Oval deep-green leaves with deep-red veins. Low, creeping growth; leaves are larger than in the following varieties.
F. verschaffeltii **'Angel Snow'.** A new introduction similar to *argyroneura* but with blotches of creamy white.
F. verschaffeltii argyroneura (Peru). Oval vivid-green leaves with white veins; flat, creeping growth.
F. verschaffeltii argyroneura minima. The above in miniature.
F. verschaffeltii pearcei*. A low creeper with bluish olive-green leaves and rose-red veins; a pretty but slower growing variety.

Filicium decipiens, Fern Tree

Fittonia verschaffeltii, Mosaic Plant

Fittonia verschaffeltii 'Angel Snow'

Fittonia verschaffeltii argyroneura, Nerve Plant

GLOXINIAS AND ALLIED PLANTS
See Sinningia, etc.

GRAPTOPHYLLUM   Acanthaceae
and PSEUDERANTHEMUM

Caricature Plant

A colourful tropical plant, seen more in Queensland than the southern States. Used as a pot plant indoors and in greenhouses. Filtered sun.

Grow: Outdoors in tropical areas, or in warm bush-houses or glasshouses in other areas.
Position indoors: Sunroom or near sunny window.
Water: Keep moist.
Soil: General Potting Mix.
Fertiliser: Complete Plant Food (dry, liquid, or foliar) monthly.
Propagation: From cuttings.
Pests and problems: Observe for scale insects.

Varieties include:

GRAPTOPHYLLUM

G. pictum. Green foliage variegated with yellow.
G. pictum **'Bronze Variegata'.** Bronze-green foliage variegated with cream and pink.

Graptophyllum pictum, Caricature Plant

Graptophyllum pictum 'Bronze Variegata'

Fittonia verschaffeltii argyroneura minima, Miniature Nerve Plant

GRAPTOPHYLLUM, etc., continued

G. pictum 'Purpurium Variegata'. Reddish foliage with purple variegation.

G. pictum 'Tricolour'. Larger green leaves with cream variegation.

Graptophyllum pictum 'Purpurium Variegata'

Graptophyllum pictum 'Tricolour'

PSEUDERANTHEMUM

P. atropurpureum 'Variegatum'* (Polynesia). A small shrub, its purple leaves splashed with green, white, and pink.

GYNURA   Compositae

Velvet Plant

The soft Velvet Plant grows quite rapidly indoors, where it is used in hanging pots and terrariums. Also called 'Purple Passion Vine'.

Grow: In glasshouses or warm summer bush-houses.

Position indoors: Sunroom or in strong light. In weaker light, the growth is too rapid and the colour poor.

Water: Keep moist.

Soil: General Potting Mix.

Fertiliser: Complete Plant Food (dry, liquid, or foliar) monthly.

Propagation: Very easy from cuttings. Multiple planting is recommended.

Pests and problems: General observation. Keep plant nipped back for compact growth.

Varieties include:

G. sarmentosa (India). A twining plant, with soft fleshy toothed leaves, covered with purple hairs, like velvet; small orange flowers.

Gynura sarmentosa, Velvet Plant

HAEMANTHUS — Amarillidaceae

Blood Lily

This spectacular flowering bulb makes a handsome indoor pot plant, while it is in flower. The foliage follows the flowering.

Grow: Outdoors in warm, sheltered positions, or in glasshouses.

Position indoors: Sunroom or near bright window. Grow outdoors after flowering has finished.

Water: Keep moist during growth period, easing back to dry for bulb.

Soil: General Potting Mix.

Fertiliser: Complete Plant Food monthly during growth period, then none until repotting.

Propagation: Seeds from pollinated flowers.

Pests and problems: General observation.

Varieties include:

H. multiflorus (Tropical Africa). A bulbous plant, flowering Dec. to Jan., with a ball of up to 100 coral-red flowers on a thick stem. Berries follow if pollinated; leaves of green spotted brown follow flowering.

H. natalensis (South Africa). Natal Paintbrush. Bulb bearing a dense head of flowers with orange styles. Leaves follow.

HEDERA — Araliaceae

Ivy or English Ivy

The English Ivy is one of the most popular plants grown, both indoors and out. Outdoors, they are used as ground cover, as self-attaching creepers for fences and buildings, and as spillover pot plants. They are hardy enough to adapt to all climates around the world. Indoors, they are one of the most popular climbing house plants.

Grow: Prefers a cool position in semi-shade, and ample moisture.

Position indoors: Good light with air movement. Considered by many to be hardy indoors. I prefer to grow the Ivy outdoors, then cut nicely-shaped lengths which soon take root in water, indoors. Keep container full, occasionally adding a few grains of soluble fertiliser, but not to excess. The cuttings may be potted-up into soil when they are of no further use indoors.

Water: Keep evenly moist, but leave none in saucer. If Ivy is growing on totem, this should also be kept moist, to attract rooting on the totem.

Soil: General Potting Mix.

Fertiliser: Complete Plant Food (dry, liquid, or foliar) monthly, or alternate with foliar.

Propagation: From cuttings, which root easily.

Pests and problems: Scale insects. Don't over-water, or leave water in saucer.

Varieties include:

H. canariensis **'Variegata'** (Canary Islands). American Ivy. A very colourful large-leafed variety, its fresh-green leaves variegated with creamy white.

Haemanthus multiflorus, Blood Lily

Haemanthus natalensis, Natal Paintbrush

Hedera canariensis 'Variegata'

HEDERA, continued

H. helix*(Europe). English Ivy. Glossy five-lobed forest-green leaves. The variety now has many cultivars.

H. helix **'California Gold'.** This self-branching and bushy variety has its light-green leaves heavily mottled with yellow.

H. helix **'Chicago Variegated'.** A densely foliaged variety with medium-sized and irregularly variegated leaves from yellow to white, or green.

H. helix **'Conglomerata'*** (Japan). Slow-growing contorted stems with closely crowded small dark-green stiff leaves.

H. helix **'Cordata'***. Small to medium-sized heart-shaped dark-green leaves on stiff, strong stems.

H. helix cristata. Holly Ivy. Twining variety with fresh-green heavily frilled and crimpled leaves.

H. helix **'Discolour'.** Small deep-green leaves mottled with white. New growth almost all white.

H. helix **'Erecta'** (Japan). Similar to *helix* 'Conglomerata', with erect stems and more pointed leaves.

H. helix **'Glacier'.** Tri-lobed medium-sized green and grey leaves, nicely variegated with white, with a pink edge in the cooler months.

Hedera helix 'California Gold'

Hedera helix 'Erecta'

Hedera helix 'Chicago Variegated'

Hedera helix cristata, Holly Ivy

Hedera helix 'Discolour'

Hedera helix 'Glacier'

140

Hedera helix 'Glacier Diamond'

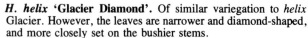

H. helix 'Glacier Diamond'. Of similar variegation to *helix* Glacier. However, the leaves are narrower and diamond-shaped, and more closely set on the bushier stems.

H. helix 'Goldust'. Tri-lobed, medium-sized leaves, variegated and mottled with green and yellow, especially on new growth.

H. helix 'Goldheart'. A neat, slender grower, with medium-sized dark-green leaves having a yellow to cream centre-marking, on red stems. A striking species.

H. helix 'Green Spear'*. Medium-green spear-shaped leaves which are long, pointed, and veined paler.

H. helix 'Maculata'*. Medium-sized roundish to five-lobed leaves, yellowish to deep green, mottled cream or white.

H. helix 'Maderiensis Variegata'*. Medium-sized green leaves, faintly edged with creamy-white, becoming pink during the cooler months.

H. helix 'Meagerii'*. The small narrow deep green leaves are tri-lobes, on freely branching stems.

H. helix 'Pedata'. Birdsfoot Ivy. Dainty, narrow-lobed deep-green leaves, with whitish veins; long, twining.

H. helix 'Pedata Variegata'*. A variegated form, the narrow, tri-lobed greyish-green leaves having a broad cream edging.

H. helix 'Pin Oak'. Needlepoint Ivy. Has tri-lobed deep green leaves, on freely branching stems.

H. helix 'Pin Oak Variegated'. Similar to the above, but heavily variegated with cream and yellow.

Hedera helix 'Pin Oak Variegated'

Hedera helix 'Goldheart'

Hedera helix 'Goldust'

Hedera helix 'Pin Oak'

Hedera helix 'Pedata'

141

HEDERA, continued

H. helix **'Pittsburgh'.** A freely branching and dainty variety with medium-sized fresh-green veined leaves.

H. helix **'Pixie'.** A dense, small but thickly growing variety, with fluted shiny leaves with 5 lobes.

H. helix **'Purpurea'*.** Medium-sized leaves, lightly veined and turning purple during winter.

H. helix **'Sagittaefolia'*.** Medium-sized bright-green leaves, heavily veined with white.

H. helix **'Shamrock'.** Medium-sized, with deep-green heavily lobed leaves.

H. helix **'Smithii'.** Medium-sized, star-like five-lobed, dark-green fluted leaves which curl at the tips.

H. helix **'Tricolor'*.** Small to medium-sized green and grey leaves, variegated with cream; pink edging in winter.

H. helix **'Webers California'.** A very dense variety with bright-green five-lobed lightly veined leaves.

H. helix **'Webers Fan'*.** Similar to Webers California, but with the deep green multi-lobed leaves heavily veined.

Hedera helix 'Pittsburgh'

Hedera helix 'Pixie'

Hedera helix 'Shamrock'

Hedera helix 'Weber's California'

142   *Hedera helix* 'Smithii'

HEIMERLIODENDRON Nyctaginaceae
Pisonia

H. brunonianum 'Variegatum' (New Zealand). This showy plant resembles a variegated rubber tree. Called a Bird Catcher Tree, because of the attraction of its seed pods to birds. The green leaves are variegated with cream, sometimes showing a tinge of pink.

Grow: Outdoors in sheltered warmth or glasshouse. Ideally suited for patio or verandah. Filtered sun.
Position indoors: Sunroom or near airy window. Keep moist and fertilise with Complete Plant Food each 2 months. Propagate by cuttings.

HEMIGRAPHIS Acanthaceae
Purple Waffle Plant

H. exotica (New Guinea). The Purple Waffle Plant. This trailing Coleus-like plant has purple foliage, with wine-red reverse. Requires warm bush-house or glasshouse. Trim back regularly to keep compact. No sun. General Potting Mix. Propagate by cuttings.

Hemigraphis exotica, Purple Waffle Plant

Heimerliodendron brunonianum 'Variegatum', Bird Catcher Tree (Pisonia)

HOFFMANNIA   Rubiaceae

Taffeta Plant

Taffeta Plants are best grown in warm glasshouses or warm summer bush-houses, and are an attractive collectors' plant.

Grow: In glasshouse or warm tropical bush-house.
Position indoors: Sunroom or near warm window, with filtered sun.
Water: Keep moist.
Soil: Indoor Potting Mix.
Fertiliser: Complete Plant Food each 1–2 months.
Propagation: From cuttings.
Pests and problems: General observation. Pinch back taller plants to keep bushy.

Varieties include:
H. ghiesbreghtii (Mexico)*. An erect plant, with 4 cornered stems, and long corrugated, drooping black-green leaves, red beneath; tubular flowers, yellow spotted red.
H. ghiesbreghtii 'Variegata'. As above, but richly variegated with cream and pink.
H. refulgens 'Vittata'. A slow growing low plant, with deep red stems, and coppery-green corrugated leaves with paler veins, reverse wine red.

Hoffmania refulgens 'Vittata', Quilted Taffeta Plant

Hoffmania ghiesbreghtii 'Variegata', Variegated Taffeta Plant

HOYA   Asclepiadaceae

Wax Plants

Wax Plants are so-called because of the beautiful heads of wax-like flowers, usually produced in spring and autumn. Some Hoyas are natives of Queensland and northern New South Wales, and are easily grown in sheltered positions, both sunny and shaded, outdoors and indoors. They are trailers which are suitable for pots or hanging baskets. The flowers should never be cut off as more will form from these flower spikes.

Grow: On warm trellis outdoors, or can be potted into 30 cm pots with suitable support or ladder. It then makes an attractive verandah or patio plant.
Position indoors: Wonderful for sunrooms, in pots or hangers, or indoors near a bright, airy window.
Water: Allow to dry between waterings.
Soil: General Potting Mix.
Fertiliser: Complete Plant Food (dry, liquid or foliar) each 1–2 months.
Propagation: From cuttings.
Pests and problems: Watch for scale or mealy bugs.

Varieties include:
H. australis (Queensland). A twining creeper with broad, oval, thick, waxy green leaves and white wax-like star flowers with a red centre.
H. bella (India). A dwarf shrubby species with small pointed leaves and white waxy flowers with a mauve centre.
H. carnosa (Queensland). Wax Flowers. A creeper with narrow green leaves in pairs, and waxy pale-pink flowers with a red centre.
H. carnosa 'Compacta'. Hindu Rope Plant. A tortured and twisted vine, which has its own fascination. Compact heads of pink flowers.
H. carnosa 'Compacta Mauna Loa' (Laura Lei). Resembling 'Exotica' variegation in the twisted form.
H. carnosa 'Compacta Regalis'. Resembling *carnosa* 'Variegata' markings in the twisted form.
H. carnosa 'Exotica'. The green leaves have a central area of cream, becoming suffused pink, with red twining runners.
H. carnosa 'Krinkle 8'. The glossy deep green leaves are puckered between the veins.

Hoya australis, Porcelain Flower

Hoya carnosa 'Krinkle 8'

Hoya bella, Miniature Wax Plant

Hoya carnosa 'Compacta Regalis', Variegated Hindu Rope

Hoya carnosa 'Compacta Mauna Loa', Laura Lei

Hoya carnosa, Wax Plant

Hoya carnosa 'Compacta', Hindu Rope Plant

Hoya carnosa 'Exotica'

HOYA, continued

H. carnosa 'Rubra' ('Krimson Princess'). Similar to 'Exotica', but new growth is red, and the leaves are oval-shaped, flowers rose.

H. carnosa 'Tricolour' ('Krimson Queen'). Similar to above, but new growth is suffused rose pink and the variegation resembling *H.c.* 'Variegata', flowers rose.

H. carnosa 'Variegata'. A beautiful variegated-foliage form, its bright-reen leaves bordered with cream and pink; flowers deep pink.

H. imperialis (Borneo). Deep green longer leaves, and red flower with cream centre.

H. longifolia (Sikkim). Has long narrow leaves, and waxy white flowers.

H. micrantha (Burma). Small leathery leaves and cream velvety flowers.

H. multiflora 'Starburst'. A regular flowerer, creamy yellow with brown centre.

H. purpureo-fusca 'Silver Pink'. Good grower with silver mottled foliage and deep red flowers.

Hoya carnosa 'Rubra', Krimson Princess

Hoya carnosa 'Tricolour', Krimson Queen

Hoya imperialis

146   *Hoya carnosa* 'Variegata'

Hoya multiflora 'Starburst'

Hoya purpureo-fusca, Silver Pink Hoya

Hoya micrantha

Hoya longifolia (Hoya longifolia shepherdii)

Hoya purpureo-fusca 'Silver Pink' – with flower

147

HYPOESTES   Acanthaceae

Freckle Face or Polka Dot Plant

Rapid-growing small plants, which need to be regularly pinched back to keep compact. They will grow in bright or filtered sun, sheltered positions outdoors, in glasshouse or bush-house, as well as bright areas indoors and sunrooms.

Water: Keep moist.
Soil: Indoor Potting Mix.
Fertiliser: Complete Plant Food or foliar fertiliser, monthly.
Propagation: From cuttings. The pinched-out cuttings will root easily. Replace plants when too lanky.
Pests and problems: None observed.

Varieties include:
H. phyllostachya (sanguinolenta) (Madagascar). Freckle Face. Small plant, green leaves spotted red.
H. phyllostachya 'Splash'. The improved Freckle Face. A soft, fast-growing plant with deep-green leaves covered with pink blotches; lilac flowers.

IMPATIENS   Balsaminaceae

Perennial Balsams

These hardy, continuous-flowering plants are bright in semi-shaded garden positions, and in pots on patios and verandahs. They may be planted in with leggy plants, to fill in the lower area. Also called Patient Lucy and Busy Lizzie.

Position indoors: In sunrooms and well-lit indoor positons.
Water: Keep evenly moist.
Soil: Indoor Potting Mix.
Fertiliser: Complete Plant Food (dry, liquid, or foliar) monthly.
Propagation: From seed or cuttings.
Pests and problems: Generally observe.

Varieties include:
I. hawkerii **hybrids.** These were discovered in New Guinea, and produce beautifully variegated leaves in gold, cream, pink, and green, as well as the various flower shades.
I. walleriana (sultani) (Zanzibar). these waxy, brittle-foliaged plants flower continually, in all shades from red, orange, and pink to white, as well as two-toned. There are many new hybrid and dwarf varieties. There are also variegated foliage and double flowered forms.

Hypoestes phyllostachya, Freckle Face

Hypoestes phyllostachya 'Splash', improved Freckle Face

Impatiens hawkerii hybrid

Impatiens walleriana, Orange-flowered – growing in a sunroom

Impatiens walleriana 'Variegata', Variegated Patient Lucy

Impatiens walleriana, Double Pink

Impatiens walleriana (sultani) mixed colours, Patient Lucy

Impatiens walleriana, Double Red

149

IPOMOEA　Convolvulaceae

Morning Glory

*I. batatus** (E. Indies). Sweet Potato Vine. Makes an attractive and economical indoor creeper. Select a sweet potato of about 10 cm in length or cut one to this length, and place it (cut-side down) in the neck of a jar of water, where it will soon grow. Nip back the ends to keep bushy. When rooted thoroughly, it may be planted in soil where it may last several years. Fertilise occasionally, and watch for spider mites.

I. horsfalliae (W. Indies). This attractive, tropical creeper, also known as Morning Glory, may be grown in tropical and sub-tropical gardens, or in cooler areas in glasshouses. The winter flowers are bells of rich waxy rose or red.

Soil: General Potting Mix.
Fertiliser: Complete Plant Food (dry, liquid, or foliar) monthly during summer.
Propagation: From cuttings, difficult.
Pests and problems: Caterpillars and spider mites.

IXORA　Rubiaceae

Flame of the Woods

Popular as potted flowering plants in temperate areas, but may be found growing in gardens in tropical and sub-tropical areas, where they come in a variety of colours.

Grow: In glasshouse and warm, summer bush-house, and as pot plants for patios and poolsides.
Position indoors: Sunroom or selected sunny window.
Water: Keep moist.
Soil: General Potting Mix.
Fertiliser: Complete Plant Food (dry, liquid, or foliar) monthly.
Propagation: From cuttings.
Pests and problems: Scale and spider mites.

Varieties include:
I. chinensis **'Fireball'** (Southern China, Malaya). A compact grower, with large heads of orange-red flowers.
I. chinensis **'Prince of Orange'**. This popular variety with stiff deep-green foliage has attractive heads of scarlet flowers.
I. compacta **'Sunkist'** (Malaya). Dwarf variety from Singapore, favouring full sun. Grows around 30 cm, with masses of small scarlet-orange flowers in heads.

Ipomea horsfalliae, Morning Glory

Ixora chinensis 'Fireball'

Ixora chinensis 'Prince of Orange'

Ixora compacta 'Sunkist'

JATROPHA Euphorbiaceae

Coral Plant

These unusual, bulbous-trunk plants may be grown in tropical or temperate gardens or as patio pot plants. The unusual foliage and continuous flowering makes them most popular.

Grow: In pots on warm, sunny patio or verandah, in most areas, or in glasshouses.
Position indoors: Requires an airy and sunny spot.
Water: Keep moist, not over-wet.
Soil: General Potting Mix.
Fertiliser: Complete Plant Food (dry, liquid, or foliar) monthly during summer.
Propagation: Collect seeds that form after flowering.
Pests and problems: General observation.

Varieties include:
J. multifida (Central America). Coral Plant. The leaves are heavily segmented, growing on bulbous trunk when juvenile. Red flowers.
J. podagrica (W. Indies, Central America). Fiddle-shaped leaves, grows to 10 cm, red flowers.

KAEMPFERIA Zingiberaceae

Dwarf Ginger Lily

These Ginger Lilies are attractive, small, and free-flowering pot plants. They are winter-dormant, but suitable for summer pots indoors.

Grow: In glasshouse or warm, summer bush-house.
Position indoors: In sunroom or near warm, but bright, airy window.
Water: Keep moist during growing period, drying out for winter dormancy.
Soil: General Potting Mix.
Fertiliser: A few grains of Complete or foliar fertilisers, monthly during summer, easing off approaching winter.
Propagation: Divide dormant pots before repotting in spring.
Pests and problems: General observation.

Varieties include:
K. gilbertii (Southern Burma). Variegated Ginger Lily. Variegated foliage and flowers with violet bands on lip.
K. pulchra (Burma). Pretty Resurrection Lily. Leaves have peacock markings. Flowers are lavender, and appear daily for many months from the one base.

Jatropha podagrica

Jatropha multifida, Coral Plant

Kaempferia pulchra, Pretty Resurrection Lily

Kaempferia gilbertii
Variegated Ginger Lily

151

KALANCHOE   Crassulaceae

These eye-catching plants are so easily grown in Australia that nurseries have not developed them to their fullest commercial potential. By controlled lighting, they can be made to flower at any desired time. This is achieved by creating 14 hours of night darkness. Flowers appear about 3 months after the long night schedule has begun.

Grow: In garden rockeries, or outdoor position. Ideal for pots on patios.
Position indoors: Any bright and airy windowsill or sunroom.
Water: Allow soil to dry out between waterings.
Soil: General Potting Mix.
Fertiliser: Complete Plant Food every 2–3 weeks until flowering and again after cutting back.
Propagation: From seed or cutting. Many different colours are available from seeds.
Pests and problems: General observation. Cut back after flowering.

Varieties include:
K. blossfeldiana **'Brilliant Star'** * (Madagascar). Extremely large flowered heads of bright-red flowers on strong, wiry stems; low base foliage of glossy green leaves.
K. blossfeldiana **'Fiery Blossom'** *. Also similar to 'Brilliant Star' in size and habit, but coppery-red in colour.
K. blossfeldiana **'Tom Thumb'**. Similar to the above, but in miniature.

LAMIUM   Labiatae

Aluminium Creeper

L. galeobdolon 'Variegatum' *(L. scandens)*. (Europe to Urals). A small trailing plant with hairy green leaves, prettily marked in silver; small, lipped, yellow flowers marked red.

Grow: As rockery creeper, or in hanging pots and baskets on patios, ferneries, or indoors.
Position indoors: Sunroom or near cool, airy window.
Water: Keep moist.
Soil: General Potting Mix.
Fertiliser: Complete Plant Food (dry, liquid, or foliar) each 1–2 months.
Propagation: From cuttings.
Pests and problems: Mealy bug.

Lamium galeobdolon 'Variegatum' *(scandens)*, Aluminium Creeper

Kalanchoe blossfeldiana 'Tom Thumb', Dwarf Kalanchoe

LEEA   Vitaceae

Hawaiian Holly

Fast becoming one of our leading indoor plants, but will not thrive in temperatures below 17°–20°C. As the temperature begins to rise above this, glossy new growth rapidly appears. The final thrill is reached when clusters of red berry-like buds appear. These open to small pink flowers.

Grow: Heated glasshouse in winter, or warm summer bush-house.
Position indoors: Thrives in any warm position receiving good light.
Water: Leeas have a big thirst. Keep constantly moist, preferably immersing pot, once or twice weekly.
Soil: General Potting Mix.
Fertiliser: Complete Plant Food.
Propagation: From seed or cuttings.
Pests and problems: Generally observe. Defoliation can be caused by intermittent watering.

Varieties include:
L. coccinea (Burma). Hawaiian Holly. Handsome green leaves with fluted serrated edges, red berries with pink petals.
L. 'Burgundy'. This deep purple-foliaged variant is a handsome plant indeed, and so new that it is not yet well known in Australia. It should become one of our leading indoor plants. The flowers are burgundy berries, which later have pink petals.

LIGULARIA   Compositae

Leopard Plant

This small clustering plant may be grown in temperate climates in the garden in filtered sunlight. Also used as a pot plant on patios and in greenhouses.

Water: Keep moist.
Soil: General Potting Mix.
Fertiliser: Complete Plant Food (dry, liquid, or foliar) every 1–2 months.
Propagation: By division.
Pests and problems: Generally observe.

Varieties include:
L. tussilaguinea argentea. The leaves of this variety are variegated with cream or white, especially at the margins.
L. tussilaguinea aureo-maculata (Japan). Farfugium or Leopard Plant. An attractive plant with round deep-green leaves, blotched with yellow and cream; light-yellow daisy-like flowers.

Leea 'Burgundy', Purple Hawaiian Holly

Ligularia tussilaguinea aureo-maculata, Leopard Plant

Ligularia tussilaguinea argentea

Leea coccinea, Hawaiian Holly

MANIHOT   Euphorbiaceae

Tapioca Plant

M. esculenta 'Variegata' (Brazil). Cassava or Tapioca Plant. This small tropical tree has vividly variegated, green and cream foliage. It may be grown outdoors in tropical gardens, in filtered sun. Otherwise in glasshouses. Winter deciduous.

Water: Keep moist.
Soil: Indoor Potting Mix.
Fertiliser: Complete Plant Food (dry, liquid, or foliar).
Propagation: From cuttings, in spring.
Pests and problems: Spider mite.

MARANTA FAMILY   Marantaceae

Calathea, Ctenanthe, Maranta, and Stromanthe

These bright plants are grown in protected garden corners and are a valuable inclusion to the indoor range.

Grow: In sheltered garden corners and bush-houses. The more delicate varieties should be grown in glasshouses.
Position indoors: In sunrooms and near bright windows. Filtered sun to bright light.
Water: Keep evenly moist during growth period.
Soil: Indoor Potting Mix.
Fertiliser: Complete Plant Food (dry, liquid, or foliar).
Propagation: By division.
Pests and problems: Watch for mealy bug.

Varieties include:

CALATHEA
Peacock Plants

C. acuminata. Has narrow, shiny leaves, olive green above, and wine red beneath, on red hairy stems.
C. argyraea (Brazil). Hard silver leaf, with dark feather design, low growth.

Manihot esculenta 'Variegata', Variegated Tapioca Plant

Calathea acuminata

Calathea argyraea,
Silver Calathea

154

Calathea auriantiaca

C. auriantiaca (Brazil). Oval leaf grey-green, with darker markings.

C. brachemiana (Brazil). A small variety, with narrow grey-green leaves with dark-green markings from the midrib.

C. concinnia (Brazil). Stiff leaf, light green, feathered dark green, maroon beneath.

C. insignus (Brazil). Narrow, stiff, upright-growing, light-green leaves with blackish markings, maroon-red beneath.

*C. lietzei** (Brazil). Narrow deep-green leaf, with lighter green feather design; purple beneath. Sends up runners with young plantlets.

C. makoyana (Brazil). Peacock Plant. A beautiful species with the design showing on both sides of the oval leaves. The markings are olive-green, reddish at the back of the leaf on a pale-green ground.

C. medio-picta (Brazil). A larger variety, with olive-green leaves, having a white-feather centre-marking; attractive short flower, white tinted with mauve.

*C. micans** (Brazil, Peru). A miniature variety with mid-green leaves having a white centre-marking.

*C. musaica** (Brazil). A beautiful low-growing species with smooth, glossy yellow-green leaves, quaintly marked in green.

*C. ornata roseo-lineata** (Central America). Narrow, oval, olive-green leaves nicely marked with closely-set pairs of rosy-red stripes in juvenile stage, turning white on maturity; purple beneath.

C. picturata 'Argentea' (Venezuela). A dwarf variety, almost entirely covered with silver except for a dark-green border; wine-red beneath.

Calathea brachemiana

Calathea insignus, Rattlesnake Plant

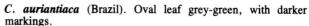

Calathea concinnia

Calathea picturata 'Argentea'

Calathea makoyana, Peacock Plant

Left: *Calathea medio-picta*. Centre: *Calathea veitchiana*. Right: *Ctenanthe setosa*

155

MARANTA FAMILY, continued

C. picturata vandenheckei (Colombia). A dwarf variety with glossy olive-green leaves, with feathered silver-white design in centre of leaf, and again towards margin; red beneath.

C. princeps (Amazon). Deep green leaf, with yellow feather design, maroon beneath.

C. roseo-picta (Brazil). A low-growing variety with large rounded deep-green leaves with red markings; red beneath.

C. roseo-picta **'Asian Beauty'** **(Ruby Star).** A beautiful new variety, with the cream leaves totally flushed in purple-red.

C. undulata (Peru). Deep green, with broad silver centre stripe. Green bracts with white flowers. Small plant.

C. veitchiana (Ecuador, Peru). A beautiful variety with large leaves marked like a peacock, in shades of green, yellow, red and brown; red beneath.

C. zebrina (Brazil). Large velvety-green leaf; midrib and veins paler green; purple beneath.

C. zebrina binottii (Brazil). Large variety, with thinner leaves, differently marked to the above. Green beneath.

Calathea roseo-picta 'Asian Beauty', Ruby Star

Calathea zebrina binottii

Calathea veitchiana, Peacock Plant

Calathea undulata

Calathea princeps

Calathea roseo-picta

Calathea zebrina, Zebra Plant

Calathea picturata vandenheckei

156

CTENANTHE

C. lubbersiana (Brazil). Oblong green leaves, variegated and mottled yellow.

C. oppenheimiana (Brazil). Tall branching growth with dark-green leaves, banded with silver and wine-red beneath.

C. oppenheimiana **'Tricolour'** (Brazil). Narrow green leaves, variegated white and pink; wine-red beneath.

C. setosa (Brazil). A thin, bushy plant with narrow green leaves banded with silver and purple beneath. (Illus. p. 155.)

Ctenanthe lubbersiana

Ctenanthe oppenheimiana 'Tricolour', Never-never Plant

Ctenanthe oppenheimiana

157

MARANTA FAMILY, continued

MARANTA
Prayer Plants

M. arundinacea 'Variegata'* (Central America). The narrow mid-green leaves are variegated or margined with white, visible through the leaf.

M. bicolour* (Brazil). Low-growing, with 15 cm oval leaves, having a grey centre feather band, surrounded by a deep green zone, and an outer grey-green band, purple beneath; flowers white, lined violet.

M. leuconeura 'Erythrophylla' (Brazil). Similar to the specie, but having a brilliant red inner veining.

M. leuconeura kerchoveana (Brazil). Prayer Plant or Ten Commandments. Low-growing with round papery green leaves and five chocolate-brown spots either side of midrib; small white flowers.

M. leuconeura kerchoveana 'Variegata'. Appears to be a sport from *kerchoveana*, and is identical except for the cream-flecked variegation all over the leaf.

M. leuconeura 'Massangeana' (Brazil). Bluish-green leaves with silver design from centre vein; red beneath; low growth.

STROMANTHE

S. amabilis (Brazil). Showy variety, stocky grower. The bright green leaves have silver markings, grey beneath. (Now renamed *Calathea amabilis*).

S. sanguinea (Calathea discolour) (Brazil). A tall, stiff grower, with long deep olive-green glossy leaves, blood-red beneath; showy head of salmon-red waxy bracts, with white flowers.

Maranta leuconeura 'Erythrophylla', Red-veined Prayer Plant

Maranta leuconeura kerchoveana, Prayer Plant

Stromanthe sanguinea (Calathea discolour)

Maranta leuconeura 'Massangeana'

Stromanthe amabilis (Calathea amabilis)

158

Maranta leuconeura kerchoveana 'Variegata', Variegated Prayer Plant

MEDINILLA — Melastomaceae

Rose Grape

M. magnifica (Philippines, Java). This is an eye-catching shrub, with large leathery leaves, and a height of up to 2 m. What makes it even more spectacular are the 30 cm pendulous spikes of pink, producing first berries then opening to flowers in spring and autumn. A collector's prize.

Grow: In tropics and subtropics Medinilla will grow outdoors in sheltered positions, otherwise in warm glasshouses.
Position indoors: Bright sunroom or any warm, well-lit position.
Water: Keep moist.
Soil: Indoor Potting Mix.
Fertiliser: Complete Plant Food each month.
Propagation: From cuttings.
Pests and problems: Mealy bug, and scale.

MONSTERA — Araceae

Swiss Cheese Plant

These close relatives of Philodendrons are widely grown as pot plants indoors. *Monstera deliciosa*, the Fruit Salad Plant, is also grown outdoors for its very tasty fruit and tropical-look foliage.

Grow: In glasshouses, bush-houses or sheltered outdoor positions, such as patios or verandahs.
Position indoors: Prefers well-lit position near a window, but hardy enough to tolerate poorer light for short periods. Best grown on totems.
Water: Keep moist. If on totem, keep this moist also.
Soil: General Potting Mix.
Fertiliser: Complete Plant Food (dry, liquid, or foliar) monthly.
Propagation: Some from seed, all from cuttings.
Pests and problems: Very few.

Varieties include:

M. deliciosa (Mexico). A stout-stemmed creeper forming long aerial roots, with large oval leaves which are cut and holed near the centre. Edible fruit is known as Tropical Fruit Salad. A miniature of this species is known as *Philodendron pertusum*.
*M. friedrichstahlii** (Costa Rica). A prolific climber with oval fresh-green leaves which if climbing upright, on a moss pole or bark, will split from the centre to the margin.
M. obliqua expilata (leichtlinii) (Brazil). Window Leaf. The split leaves remain joined at the edges.

Medinilla magnifica, Rose Grape

Monstera deliciosa, Tropical Fruit Salad

Monstera obliqua expilata (leichtlinii), Window Leaf

MUEHLENBECKIA and HOMALOCLADIUM   Polygonaceae

These plants, with their distinctive and unusual appearance, are strangely attractive.

Grow: In sheltered areas outdoors, in bush-houses and glasshouses.

Position indoors: In sunroom or near an airy window. Bright light to filtered sun. Hardy.

Water: Keep moist.

Soil: General Potting Mix.

Fertiliser: Complete Plant Food (dry, liquid, or foliar).

Propagation: From cuttings.

Pests and problems: General observation.

Varieties include:

Muehlenbeckia complexa (New Zealand). Wire Vine or Maidenhair Vine. A hardy basket vine with tough wiry stems, and greenish-white flowers.

Homalocladium platycladum (now renamed *Muehlenbeckia*) (Solomon Islands). Ribbon Bush or Centipede Plant. An unusual plant with flat fresh-green stems in sections, and small leaves.

NEMATANTHUS (HYPOCYRTA)   Gesneriaceae

Gold Fish Plant

This shiny, green-leafed relative of Columneas has wax-like flowers. It may be grown in glasshouses or similar. Warmth but no direct sun.

Position indoors: Sunroom or near bright, warm window.

Water: Keep moist.

Soil: Indoor Potting Mix.

Fertiliser: Complete Plant Food or foliar fertiliser monthly.

Propagation: From cuttings.

Pests and problems: General observation.

Varieties include:

N. **'Castinet'.** Has shiny green leaves, which are red beneath, except for a green margin. Apricot flowers.

N. glabra (wettsteinii) (Brazil). Clog Plant or Gold Fish Plant. This small shiny green basket plant has small waxy orange flowers.

N. **'Moonglow'.** Has glossy, green leaves which are very reflective, and red-marked yellow flowers.

N. **'Tropicana'.** Has shiny bronzy-green leaves and yellow-mottled red waxy flowers.

Nematanthus 'Castinet'

Nematanthus 'Moonglow'

Muehlenbeckia complexa, Wire Vine

Homalocladium (Muehlenbeckia) platycladum, Ribbon Bush or Centipede Plant

160

Nematanthus glabra (wettsteinii), Clog Plant

OXALIS   Oxalidaceae

Fire Fern

It may seem strange to think of cultivating Oxalis, when so many gardeners are looking for ways of eliminating another variety, which is such a nuisance, but this quaint little plant has an attraction of its own.

Grow: In a glasshouse or warm summer bush-house.

Position indoors: Sunroom or near a warm but airy window.

Water: Allow to dry between waterings.**Soil:** General Potting Mix.

Fertiliser: Complete Plant Food or foliar fertiliser each 1–2 months.

Propagation: From cuttings.

Pests and problems: Spider mites.

Varieties include:

O. hedysaroides rubra **'Fire Fern'** (N.W. South America). An erect shrubby plant, with thin stems bearing wine-red oval leaves, in threes; contrasting yellow flowers.

Oxalis hedysaroides rubra, Firefern

Nematanthus 'Tropicana'

161

PALMS   Palmae

My earliest childhood memories of indoor plants, long
before they became fashionable in the home, were of Kentia
palms in the foyer of the local theatre. Then there were the
large *Phoenix canariensis* palms that we used to play under in
my grandparents' garden. These days no indoor plant display
or garden setting would be complete without a palm or two to
set if off.

While many palms grow on a single trunk, with their foliage
up above, there are also many which form a cluster of trunks,
so giving a denser pot plant or garden specimen. This look
may also be achieved with the single-trunked varieties by
planting them in clusters of 3 or 4. The indoor life span of
many palms, such as the Alexander, may be increased by
multiple plantings, as the browning tips (which come from
too little light for this variety) may be trimmed off with
scissors, still leaving an abundance of foliage, before they
eventually have to be moved outside again. Cluster plantings
thus increase the range of varieties of palms which may be
used indoors. Remember that many palms are rain-forest
plants, and humidity-loving, and will benefit when taken
indoors, from a regular misting or washing down of the
foliage with water. This will also keep the leaves clean and
shiny.

Kentias have in the past been the safe and long-lasting palm,
but also the most expensive. Perhaps clustering of cheaper,
more plentiful varieties may be an acceptable alternative.
Other proven, long-lasting, and hardy indoor varieties
include Rhapis, Chamaedorea, Ptychosperma, Laccaspadix
and Golden Canes. I have also had success with Phoenix,
Cocos, Archontophoenix, Caryotas, Livistona, Licuala, and
Euterpe, and I feel sure that as many others are tried out, they
will also be successful. Nothing is more softening and
relaxing for indoor decor than a palm tree.

ARCHONTOPHOENIX
Alexander and Bangalow Palms

These handsome palms are widely grown in gardens along
the east coast of Australia north of Sydney, and are one of
the most widely sold potted palms. Try multiple planting in
groups of 3–4 in pot or garden. Their variety species still
needs further sorting, but a number of varieties have been
classified; others will be listed only as hybrids. Leaves are
self-cleaning.

Grow: In tropical, subtropical, and temperate gardens or in
bush-houses, also on verandahs and patios.
Position indoors: Requires good light in an airy position
indoors or sunroom.
Water: Outdoors keep wet. Prefers timed sprinklers once
or twice daily. Indoors, allow soil to dry between
waterings, but do not neglect or keep constantly dry.
Soil: General Potting Mix.
Fertiliser: Complete Plant Food each 1–2 months.
Propagation: From seeds, which germinate in less than 2
months.
Pests and problems: Caterpillars and spider mite. Take
outdoors at first sign of distress.

Varieties include:
A. alexandrae (Queensland). Alexander Palm, also called 'King
Palm'. A handsome broad trunk with close rings, green crown
shaft and green leaves which are silver beneath. Cream flowers
and red seeds.

A. alexandrae var. 'Mount Lewis' (Queensland). Resembling
alexandrae. However the crown shaft is deep rust-brown and the
leaves broader and of thicker texture, silver beneath. Mauve
flowers, large 20-22 mm seeds.
A. alexandrae var. 'Kuranda'* (Queensland). Another distinctly different variety, with broader trunk at the base, and
handsome flower and seed skirt. Seeds have a rough, hairy
covering.
A. alexandrae var. 'Beatricae'* (Queensland). This variety has
the trunk broader at the base and stepped at the rings. Leaves are a
little more upright.
A. cunninghamiana (eastern Australia). Bangalow Palm.
Narrower trunk and rings further apart than *alexandrae*, crown
shaft is yellow-green and leaves all green. Mauve flowers and red
seeds.
A. cunninghamiana hybrid. This specie originated at Dellows
Nursery and is now to be found growing in the Gold Coast area. It
has a broader trunk, with rings closer. Leaves more upright with
yellow to brownish ribs.

ARECA — See CHRYSALIDOCARPUS

Archontophoenix alexandrae – with seeds

Archontophoenix cunninghamiana,
Bangalow Palm (juvenile form) ▶

Archontophoenix alexandrae, Alexander Palms – growing in Singapore

ARECASTRUM
Cocos Plumosa Palm

A. romanzoffianum (Brazil). The Queen Palm. A widely grown and hardy palm, suitable outdoors for all but the cooler areas, and used indoors where ceilings are high enough. Juvenile leaves are broad and unsplit, but begin to divide when 1.5–2 m. Adult leaves are arching and are a deep, glossy-green in narrow segments. The trunk is rough at first, later smooth. Edible orange fruit. Older leaves should be cut off.

Grow: Outdoors, in large pots in full to filtered sun.
Position indoors: Bright light to filtered sun.
Water: Keep evenly moist.
Soil: General Potting Mix.
Fertiliser: Complete Plant Food every 1–2 months.
Propagation: From seed, very slow germinating. Plant outdoors and forget them.
Pests and problems: Caterpillars roll the leaves. Move outdoors if distressed.

Archontophoenix alexandrae 'Mount Lewis', Mount Lewis Alexander Palm

Arecastrum romanzoffianum, Cocos Plumosa Palm

Archontophoenix cunninghamiana hybrid, Hybrid Bangalow Palm

163

BUTIA
Wine Palm

This hardy specie is known as the Wine Palm because of the fruit being used in wine-making. The stiff, broad trunk carries recurring fronds of bluish-green foliage. Large bunches of yellow fruit. Mostly used as an outdoor palm or large tub specimen, requiring bright sun and ample water. Seeds are slow to germinate.

Varieties include:
B. capitata (Brazil). The Jelly or Wine Palm. Grey-green leaves and 2-cm fruit.
B. yatay (Argentina). The Yatay Palm. Taller trunk, with bluish-grey leaves and 4-cm fruit.

CARYOTA
Fishtail Palm

These unusual palms are liked very much by some and disliked by others. The leaf formation is very eye-catching, particularly when seen spread overhead against the sky.

Grow: Outdoors in warmer climates north of Sydney, and excellent as a large pot plant indoors and on patios.
Position indoors: Bright light to filtered sun.
Water: Keep evenly moist.
Soil: General Potting Mix.
Fertiliser: Complete Plant Food every 1–2 months.
Propagation: From seed. After seed collection, the trunk (or tree if single-stemmed) dies.
Pests and problems: Watch for scale insects. Move outdoors at first sign of distress.

Varieties include:
C. mitis (E. Indies). Clustered Fishtail Palm. A handsome garden specimen, more resembling a bushy tree than a palm. Red fruit on shorter stems of half a metre.
C. urens* (India, Sri Lanka). Fishtail Palm. A handsome single-trunked specimen. Red fruit on long stems of 3–4 m.

Butia capitata, Jelly or Wine Palm

Caryota mitis, Clustered Fishtail Palm

Caryota mitis (juvenile form)

Butia yatay, Yatay Palm

CHAMAEDOREA
Parlour Palm

This selection of small shade-loving palms is highly-prized for its indoor hardiness. Most are at home in small pots, even goblets, bottles, and terrariums and may be gradually potted-on, until they occupy a larger pot. If grown outdoors they should be kept away from sun, as strong light will yellow the foliage.

Grow: In glasshouses, warm bush-houses, sheltered verandah or garden.
Position indoors: Bright to poorer-lit areas.
Water: Keep moist, not over-wet.
Soil: General Potting Mix.
Fertiliser: Complete Plant Food (nothing containing urea).

Propagation: From seed.
Pests and problems: Generally observe.

Varieties include:
C. elegans (Neanthe bella) (Mexico, Guatemala). Parlour Palm. Small dainty palm to 1 m, flowers with small yellow berries when quite young.
C. erumpens (Honduras). Bamboo Palm. Has multiple trunks to 3 m, leaf segments are broader at the ends. Makes a handsome pot plant.
C. metallica (Mexico). Miniature Fishtail Palm. To 1 m with unsplit leaves of unusual design.
C. seifrizii (Mexico). Reed Palm or Clustered Parlour Palm. To 2–3 m. Similar to *erumpens* but leaves are narrower. Excellent indoors and withstands more sun than others.

CHRYSALIDOCARPUS (ARECA)
Golden Cane Palm

Graceful, cane-trunked palms, single or clustered, for warmer gardens north of Sydney, and excellent as indoor potted palms.

Grow: In glasshouses, warm bush-houses, or sheltered, warm, semi-shaded areas.
Position indoors: Warm with filtered sun or bright light.
Water: Keep soil wet, but do not stand in water.
Soil: General Potting Mix.
Fertiliser: Complete Plant Food, monthly during summer.
Propagation: From seed.
Pests and problems: Watch for scale and mealy bug.

Varieties include:
*C. lucubensis** (Madagascar). Grows to 10 m on single trunk, leaf appearance not unlike *Arecastrum*. Lime green trunk.
C. lutescens (Madagascar). Golden Cane or Butterfly Palm. This graceful palm to 6 m on golden multiple trunks has attractive foliage of green but yellowing in full sunlight. Highly prized indoors.

Chamaedorea elegans (Neanthe bella), Parlour Palm

Chamaedorea erumpens, Bamboo Palm

Chamaedorea metallica, Miniature Fishtail Palm

Chamaedorea seifrizii, Reed Palm or Clustered Fishtail Palm

Chrysalidocarpus lutescens, Golden Cane Palm – in Mandarin Hotel, Singapore

165

DICTYOSPERMA
Princess Palm

Grows to 10 m and resembles *Archontophoenix,* with the first noticeable differences being the vertical slits, and more slender, grey trunk, and the freshly opening leaf being held from splitting by a border of foliage. Growing conditions would be similar to *Archontophoenix.*

D. album (Mauritius). Princess Palm. Blackish-grey trunk, green crown shaft and whitish-green leaves. Large reddish-yellow flowers and purplish seeds.
***D. album* var. *rubrum*.** Similar to *album* but the young plants have leaves which are darker and with red veins. Flowers are yellow.

Dictyosperma album, Princess Palm

Chrysalidocarpus lutescens, Golden Cane Palm – at Dellow's Nursery, Southport, Qld.

COCOS
Coconut Palm

See also *Arecastrum* and *Microcoelum*

C. nucifera (Most tropical islands). Coconut Tree. To 30 m on slender trunks, will grow and fruit in coastal gardens north from the Gold Coast. Does not appear to be used as an indoor palm, but will grow in a glasshouse until too tall. Requires filtered sun; keep soil wet.

Dictyosperma album var. *rubrum,* Red Princess Palm

Cocos nucifera, Coconut Palm

166

EUTERPE
Assai Palm

E. edulis (Brazil). This slender palm to 20 m has a prominent green crown shaft and drooping leaves. Some plants have clustering trunks. They require filtered sun and evenly moist soil. *Euterpe* have been tried indoors quite successfully but further information is needed. Select a position with good light, keep evenly moist, but not over-wet. Use Complete Plant Food every 1–2 months, and move outdoors at first sign of distress.

Fertiliser: Complete Plant Food every 1–2 months.
Propagation: From seed. Very slow germination.
Pests and problems: Scale insects and leaf grubs.

Varieties include:
H. belmoreana (Lord Howe Island). Sentry Palm. To 8 m, on single trunk. The broad arched leaves have numerous narrow segments.
H. forsteriana (Lord Howe Island). Kentia or Paradise Palm. Grows 10–15 m on single trunk. Handsome broad leaves standing more upright than *belmoreana*. The backbone of the plant rental industry.

Howeia (Kentia) belmoreana, Sentry Palm

Euterpe edulis, Assai Palm

HOWEIA
Kentia Palm

Howeia or Kentia Palms are the most widely used indoor palms. These natives of Lord Howe Island also make fine garden specimens, with their deep grey trunks covered with a plumage of broad leaves. Filtered sun is best.

Grow: Best in glasshouse or warm bush-house.
Position indoors: Being hardy, they will tolerate poorer light for short periods, but grow best in brighter areas.
Water: Keep evenly moist.
Soil: General Potting Mix.

Howeia (Kentia) forsteriana, Kentia Palm or Paradise Palm

167

LACCASPADIX
Atherton Table Palm

L. australasica (northern Queensland). This newcomer from the Atherton Tablelands is showing great promise, as a rival to Kentias for hardiness indoors. It may also be grown outdoors in bright light or shade, and good specimens exist in Sydney Botanical Gardens. Juvenile growth is similar in appearance to *H. fosteriana* but leaves are narrower. It later clusters and grows to about 3–4 m with older growth dying to be replaced by new growth. Yellow flower and small red fruit.

Grow: In glasshouse or warm bush-house.
Position indoors: Bright to medium light.
Water: Keep evenly moist, but not over-wet.
Soil: General Potting Mix.
Fertiliser: Complete Plant Food every 1–2 months.
Propagation: From seed.

Laccaspadix australasica, Atherton Table Palm

LICUALA
Ruffled Fan Palm

These small fan palms are widely used in the tropics as decorative garden specimens, and can be seen in most hotel foyers and plant boxes. Stocks have never been plentiful in Australia, but recently small numbers have appeared, and these should be an attractive addition where humidity is high enough.

Grow: In heated glasshouse and later move into a tropical bush-house.
Position indoors: Warm, humid, brightly lit position.
Water: Keep evenly moist, and regularly mist foliage.
Soil: General Potting Mix.
Fertiliser: Complete Plant Food monthly during summer.
Propagation: From seed.

Varieties include:
L. grandis (New Britain). The most eye-catching palm grown. The pleated, soft green leaves form a full circle. Grows to 2 m. Difficult to grow but very beautiful.

Licuala grandis, Ruffled Fan Palm – in Malaysia

LIVISTONA
Fan Palm

The Fan Palms are quite popular as garden specimens in most areas of Australia, or as indoor plants, or tub specimens for pool-side or patio. They prefer filtered sunlight when in pots, but some garden specimens grow as high as 20 m.

Position indoors: Bright light to filtered sun.
Water: Keep moist.
Soil: General Potting Mix.
Fertiliser: Complete Plant Food every 1–2 months.
Propagation: From seed.
Pests and problems: Caterpillars. Remove outdoors at first sign of distress.

Varieties include:

L. australis (eastern Australia). Cabbage Tree Palm. Slender trunk to 20 m, matured leaves circular in outline and very split and drooping at tips. Juvenile plants resemble *Rhapis*. Fruit reddish-brown.

L. chinensis (southern China). Chinese Fan Palm. Grows 6–8 m on thick trunk. Leaves are wide fans heavily split and drooping at the ends. Fruit is metallic blue.

Livistona chinensis (juvenile form),
Chinese Fan Palm

MASCARENA
Bottle or Spindle Palm

Mascarenas are reasonably hardy, considering their tropical origin.

Varieties include:

*M. verschaffeltii** (Mauritius). Spindle Palm. This very handsome palm grows to 6-9 m on a tall bottle-shaped trunk. The leaf stem and ribs are golden. The flower spikes appear on the trunk below the long crown shaft. Fragrant flowers and black seeds. If taken indoors select a bright to filtered sunny position. Keep moist. Propagation is by seeds, which germinate in about 2 months.

M. lagenicaulis (Mascarene Island). Bottle Palm. Similar to the above, with a different trunk shape.

Livistona australis, Cabbage Tree Palm

Livistona chinensis, Chinese Fan Palm

Mascarena lagenicaulis, Bottle Palm – in Singapore

169

MICROCOELUM
Baby Cocos Palm

M. weddeliana (Formerly Cocos or Syagrus) (Brazil). Dwarf Cocos. A dainty palm, often sold in small pots as Feather Palm. It eventually grows to 5 m. Flowers are yellow and fruit is orange.

Grow: In outdoor gardens or bush-houses; is quite satisfactory as a pot plant.
Position indoors: Requires good light, and is very dainty despite annoying tip-burn.
Water: Keep moist.
Soil: General Potting Mix.
Fertiliser: Complete Plant Food (dry, liquid, or foliar) every 2 months.
Propagation: From seed (slow).

Phoenix canariensis, Canary Island Date Palm

Phoenix roebelenii, Dwarf Date Palm

Microcoelum (Syagrus) weddeliana, Baby Cocos Palm

PHOENIX
Date Palm

Date Palms are widely used both indoors as well as out in the garden. Some are rather tall-growing *(canariensis)* and require plenty of space, while others *(roebelenii)* are very adaptable for pot-growing indoors, or on patios, or outdoors around pool areas.

Grow: Either in pots or planted in garden.
Position indoors: Good light essential. *Canariensis* is dangerously thorny, and should be placed well back from walk-ways.
Water: Keep moist.
Soil: General Potting Mix.
Fertiliser: Outdoors, feed every 2 months with Complete Plant Food, and when indoors, with foliar fertiliser, every 2–3 weeks.
Propagation: From seed. Takes up to 2 months to germinate.

Varieties include:
P. canariensis (Canary Islands). Tall-growing, on a heavy trunk. Leaf stems are heavy and very spined and require removing for better appearance. Juvenile stage used indoors. Orange fruit in heavy clusters.
P. roebelenii (Assam to Vietnam). Dwarf Date. Very graceful and dainty. Eventually grows on a slim trunk to 2–3 m.

PTYCHOSPERMA
Solitaire Palm

This variety of palm appears to have the tips of its leaves cut off, giving it a rough look. The leaves are also subject to splitting and marking. If they had a tidier appearance, they would be highly popular, as they are among the hardiest of indoor palms, and have a rich green colouring which is bright indoors.

Position indoors: Good light is best.
Water: Keep moist.
Soil: General Potting Mix.
Fertiliser: Complete Plant Food every 2 months. In addition, use foliar each 2–3 weeks if indoors.

Varieties include:
P. elegans (Queensland). Solitaire Palm. Grows moderately tall, on a slender trunk, to 7 m. Green crown shaft, white flowers, red fruit. Good indoors.
P. macarthuri (New Guinea). A clustering palm, forming a compact cluster to about 3 m. Widely used overseas for indoor deocration. Flowers yellowish and white, fruit green to yellow, then red.

Ptychosperma elegans, Solitaire Palm

Ptychosperma macarthuri, Hurricane Palm

RHAPIS
Lady Palm

These are the most sought-after indoor palms, commanding very high prices. Their daintily segmented leaves are borne on brown fibre-covered trunks, eventually becoming very clustered. Highly prized indoors, and hardy if given sufficient light. If not, tips of leaves will die off. The two varieties are very mixed because of cross-pollination, and not easy to distinguish. Also called 'Chinese Good Luck Palm'.

Position indoors: Require good light to filtered sun. (Too much light yellows the leaves.)
Water: Keep soil wet but empty saucers.
Soil: Indoor Potting Mix.
Fertiliser: Complete Plant Food every 2 months. Use foliar every 2–3 months if indoors.

Varieties include:
R. excelsa (Southern China). Leaves are divided into 5–10 segments which are widely spaced and have an appearance of ends being chopped off. The brown fibre-covered trunks form a cluster usually 1–2 m but will eventually grow to 3 m.
R. humilis (Southern China). The leaves are smaller than *excelsa* with more segments (9–20) closer together. Leaves are more pointed and the plant has a more compact appearance, but the brown fibre-clustered trunks eventually grow 2–3 m.

ROYSTONEA
Royal Palm

Royal Palms are among the most handsome grown, principally because of the showy, smooth, grey trunks. They are especially regal when viewed in a row or used to line either side of a driveway or park walk-way. They are rarely used as indoor plants, there being other palms of more appropriate juvenile size.

Grow: In warmer climates, and provide plenty of water. Use Complete Plant Food every 2 months. Seed germinates within 2 months.

Varieties include:
*R. oleracea** (Trinidad, northern South America). The Caribbean Royal Palm. Grows on handsome trunk to 30 m. The leaves are held above crown shaft level.
R. regia (Cuba). Cuban Royal Palm. Grows on an appealingly handsome trunk to 20 m. The head of leaves is full and descends below the crown shaft level.

Rhapis humilis, Slender Lady Palm

Rhapis excelsa, Large Lady Palm

Roystonea regia, Cuban Royal Palm

171

PALMS, continued

SABAL
Palmetto Palm

Sabals are hardy outdoor palms, eventually growing on a tall trunk, in a manner similar to the Cabbage Tree palms of most areas. They eventually attain heights from 7–15 m. Seeds usually germinate within 2 months, but plants are slow-growing.

Varieties include:
S. palmetto (S.W. Coast, U.S.A.). Cabbage Palm or Palmetto. Bluish-green fan-shaped leaves, recurving and hanging. White flowers and blackish fruit.
S. texana (Texas, Mexico). Texas Palmetto. Stiff appearance, when young. Blue-green twisted fan leaves on golden stems. White flowers, brown fruit.

Sabal palmetto, Cabbage Palm or Palmetto

Sabal texana, Texan Palmetto

WASHINGTONIA
Cotton Palm

W. robusta (N.W. Mexico). Called Cotton Palm because the green fan-shaped leaves are covered in white cotton. This sturdy palm grows on a thick trunk, is fast-growing, and hardy. The leaf stems which have large cruel spines are not self-cleaning and have to be removed. Hardy everywhere, needing little attention. Seed germinates within 2 months.

Washingtonia robusta, American Cotton Palm or Mexican Fan Palm

PANDANUS   Pandanaceae
Screw Pines

Screw Pines are so-named because the foliage eventually spirals around the trunk in a corkscrew appearance. The leaves, when in full colour variegation, are handsome indeed. A very hardy pot plant for warmer temperatures.

Grow: Outdoors in tropics and subtropics or in a glasshouse in cooler areas.
Position indoors: Near a warm, bright, airy window, or sunroom.
Water: Allow to dry out between waterings. Hose plant occasionally, but allow plant to dry out at the base, before taking indoors again.
Soil: General Potting Mix.
Fertiliser: Complete Plant Food monthly, during growth.
Propagation: Remove the larger side suckers that have roots on.
Pests and problems: General observation.

Varieties include:
P. baptistii (New Britain). Blue-green with yellow stripes on margin.
P. 'Golden Pygmy'. New variety noticed recently in Singapore, massed in garden beds and growing 50 cm tall. Narrow green leaves edged in gold.
P. sanderii roehrsianus (Polynesia). The juvenile leaves of this variety are creamish-yellow. Edged green, contrasting with the older deep-green leaves.
P. veitchii (Polynesia). Narrow green leaves, striped with white and with saw-like edging.

172

Pandanus baptistii, Blue Screw Pine

Pandanus veitchii, Variegated Screw Pine

Pandanus, 'Golden Pygmy' – in Singapore

Pandanus sanderii roehrsianus, Variegated Screw Pine

PELARGONIUM   Geraniaceae

Geraniums

Geraniums are widely grown, the world over. They vary from the colourful zonal-leaf types, originating from South Africa and highly-bred by horticulturalists, to vividly coloured flowering Regals, and fragrant-leafed varieties, to climbing Ivy Geraniums. All have their honoured place in our gardens and homes.

Grow: In gardens, greenhouses and glasshouses, everywhere.
Position indoors: In bright sunrooms, or near airy, bright, sunny windows, indoors, for limited periods. Spell outdoors when looking seedy.
Water: Allow to dry out between waterings.
Soil: General Potting Mix.
Fertiliser: Complete Plant Food (dry, liquid, or foliar) monthly.
Propagation: Cuttings take root readily.
Pests and problems: Rust, and observe generally.

Varieties include:
P. fragrans **'Variegatum'.** Variegated Nutmeg Geranium, low and compact, with small rounded green leaves, irregularly variegated white, and strongly scented of nutmeg.
P. graveolens **'Lady Plymouth'.** A vigorous scented variety, with grey-green heavily serrated leaves edged with cream; small mauve flowers.

Pelargonium fragrans 'Variegatum', Variegated Nutmeg Geranium

Pelargonium graveolens 'Lady Plymouth', Variegated Rose Geranium

173

PELARGONIUM, continued

P. hortorum 'Bronze Beauty'*. Greenish-yellow leaf with chocolate zone; single pink flower.

P. hortorum 'Caroline Schmidt'. A compact grower with grey-green leaves edged white; attractive double red flowers.

P. hortorum 'Crystal Palace Gem'*. Yellow leaf with green butterfly centre-marking; single red flower.

P. hortorum 'Distinction'*. Green leaf with black ring; dark-red flower.

P. hortorum 'Dolly Varden'. Greyish-green leaf with reddish zone and cream edging; single red flower.

P. hortorum 'Golden Harry Hieover'*. Dwarf variety, gold leaf and dark-red zone; single bright-red flower.

P. hortorum 'Happy Thought'. Bright-green leaf with cream butterfly centre and splashed with brown; single red flower.

P. hortorum 'Leonie Holbrook'. Dwarf variety of green leaf, zoned with black, single red flowers.

P. hortorum 'Madame Salleron'*. A small plant, freely branching, with small green leaves bordered with white. Used as a small border plant in gardens or as a pot plant; non-flowering.

Pelargonium hortorum 'Caroline Schmidt'

Pelargonium hortorum 'Dolly Varden'

Pelargonium hortorum 'Leonie Holbrook'

Pelargonium hortorum 'Happy Thought'

Pelargonium hortorum 'Marschal McMahon'

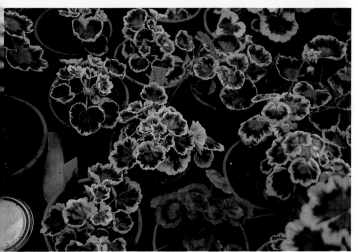

P. *hortorum* 'Marschal McMahon'. Golden yellow leaf with rich bronze zone; single scarlet flower.
P. *hortorum* 'Miss Burdette Coutts'. A beautiful compact variety, with rounded greyish-green leaves marked with ivory-white and centre zoning red; single red flower.
P. *hortorum* 'Mrs Churchill'. Green leaf, variegated with white; double pink flower.
P. *hortorum* 'Mrs Cox'*. Roundish tricoloured leaves, greyish-green in centre with a rosy-red zone and creamy yellow edging; single salmon flower.
P. *hortorum* 'Mrs Parker'*. A compact grower with grey-green leaves edged with white; double deep-pink flowers.
P. *hortorum* 'Mrs Pollock'. The tricoloured leaves are green, marked with yellow, with a brown zone, splashed with red; single red flower.
P. *hortorum* 'Mrs Quilter'*. Roundish yellowish leaves with banding of brown; orange-pink flowers.
P. *hortorum* 'Skies of Italy'. Maple-like leaves with pointed lobes, green with bronze zone, tinted orange and red, and creamy edging; single scarlet flowers.
P. *peltatum* 'Crocodile'. Ivy Geranium. Green leaves beautifully netted with gold, single cerise flowers.
P. *peltatum* 'L'Elegante'*. Ivy Geranium. Green leaves edged with white, later with pink border; single pale-pink flower.
P. *peltatum* 'Salem'*. Ivy Geranium. Mid-green leaves edged and variegated with ivory and cream; small pink flowers.
P. *peltatum* 'Sunset'*. Ivy Geranium. Green leaves unusually marked with yellow and gold; small pink flowers.
P. *peltatum* 'Variegated'*. A pleasing variety, its smooth, yellowish-green leaves having an attractive red zone; cerise flowers.
P. 'Prince Rupert' variegated*. Small, crinkled, green and cream variegated leaves, on long trailing stems; tiny lilac flowers.

Top left: *Pelargonium hortorum* 'Skies of Italy'. Left: 'Miss Burdette Coutts'. Right: 'Mrs Pollock'

Pelargonium hortorum 'Mrs Churchill'

Pelargonium peltatum 'Crocodile'

175

PELLIONIA   Urticaceae

Trailing Watermelon Begonia

This small plant resembles the Wandering Jew family, and is best grown as a ground cover or hanging pot plant.

Grow: In shade, diffused light, or filtered sun in glasshouse or warm summer bush-house.
Position indoors: Ideal in sunroom, or terrarium, or indoors near a brightly lit window.
Water: Keep on moist side, but not over-wet.
Soil: General Potting Mix.
Fertiliser: Use Complete Plant Food (half strength) or foliar fertiliser, monthly.
Propagation: Cuttings take root readily.
Pests and problems: Watch for mealy bug and spider mite.

Varieties include:
P. daveauana (Malaya). Ground or basket creeper resembling Wandering Jew, with brown-purple leaves with green to grey centre-marking.
P. pulchra (Indo-China). Smaller species with greenish leaf netted with brown veins and purple beneath.

PEPEROMIAS AND PIPERS   Piperaceae

Watermelon Begonias

Originally known as Watermelon Begonias by the introduction of *P. sandersii*. Since then there have been numerous additions, but the name has stuck. These small pot plants come in a very wide range of varieties, and are one of our most popular indoor plants. No collector would be satisfied without a dozen of these interesting gems.

Grow: In a glasshouse or warm, covered bush-house.
Position indoors: Select a warm well-lit position indoors or in a sunroom. Some varieties prefer hanging pots, others are good table specimens, while the smaller varieties and more tender ones may be best grown in lit terrariums.
Water: Do not over-water. Thoroughly moisten (preferably immerse pot) and allow to dry, before re-watering. The fine roots are easily damaged by being too wet.
Soil: General Potting Mix.
Fertiliser: Apply Complete Plant Food sparingly, or use foliar fertiliser every 2–3 weeks during summer.
Propagation: Grown from stem cuttings, others from leaf cuttings.
Pests and problems: General observation. Observe watering details.

Varieties include:
P. angulata (Venezuela, Brazil). Small upright variety, oval green leaves with parallel white stripes, on red stems.

Pellionia daveauana, Trailing Watermelon Begonia

Pellionia pulchra, Satin Pellionia

Peperomia angulata

Peperomia 'Autumn Leaf'

P. *arifolia litoralis* (Brazil). Sweetheart. Similar to *verschaffelti*, but more heart-shaped and of heavier texture.

P. 'Autumn Leaf'. Resembling *caperata*, with a mottling of cream and green. New introduction.

P. *caperata* 'Bronze Ripple'. Of similar habit and shape to Emerald Ripple, but the stems and leaves are reddish-bronze in colour.

P. *caperata* 'Emerald Ripple' (Brazil). Dwarf species forming dense clusters of roundish or heart-shaped, deeply corrugated, black-green leaves with a pale-green reverse.

P. *caperata* 'Little Fantasy'* (Brazil). Miniature species of above variety.

P. *caperata* 'Red Ripple'. An attractive new release, bronze red on shiny green leaves.

Peperomia caperata 'Emerald Ripple'

Peperomia arifolia litoralis, Sweetheart Peperomia

Peperomia caperata 'Red Ripple'

Peperomia caperata 'Bronze Ripple'

PEPEROMIA, continued

P. caperata **'Tricolour'.** This beautiful, striking form has the corrugated green leaves broadly margined with creamy-white, and red spreading out along the veins from the base.
P. clusiaefolia (West Indies). Stocky slow-growing species with thick, stiff, oval, deep-green leaves with red edging.
P. clusiaefolia **'Variegata'.** The green and red leaves are beautifully variegated with cream and red.
P. fosterii (Brazil). An attractive hanging variety, with oval fresh-green leaves having light-green parallel veins.
P. glabella (Central America). An erect branching, lightly trailing plant with waxy fresh-green leaves; reddish stems.
P. glabella **'Variegata'.** Similar to *glabella* with its light-green leaves bordered with creamy-white.

Peperomia glabella 'Variegata', Variegated Wax Privet

Peperomia clusiaefolia, Red-edged Peperomia

Peperomia clusiaefolia 'Variegata'

Peperomia glabella, Wax Privet

Peperomia caperata 'Tricolour'

Peperomia fosterii

P. **'Golden Gate'.** Attractively mottled with cream and green, on red stems. New introduction.

P. *griseo-argentea (hederaefolia)* (Brazil). A dwarf glossy silver-leafed variety.

P. *griseo-argentea* **'Blackie'.** Blackish green leaves with grey reverse.

P. *incana* (Brazil). Resembles a succulent with grey-green stiff heart-shaped leaves covered with white felt.

P. *marmorata* **'Silver Heart'** (S. Brazil). The thin, rich green, heart-shaped leaves are shaded with silver between the veins.

P. *metallica* (Peru). Showy plant in metallic bronze-green and showing a silver-green centre band.

P. *obtusifolia** (Venezuela). Robust growth, with stiff, glossy, bright-green leaves with sunken veins; stem is brownish.

P. *obtusifolia* **'Alba'.** The leaves are entirely cream.

P. *obtusifolia* **'Albo-marginata'.** A bushy grower, its fleshy green leaves variegated with cream, and having a milky hue.

Peperomia 'Golden Gate'

eperomia incana, Felted Pepperface

Peperomia griseo-argentea (hederaefolia), Ivy Peperomia

Peperomia griseo-argentea 'Blackie'

eperomia marmorata 'Silver Heart'

Peperomia metallica

Peperomia obtusifolia 'Albo-marginata'

PEPEROMIA, continued

***P. obtusifolia* 'Royal Gold'.** Differs only from the above by the distinct shape of the variegation.

***P. obtusifolia* 'Variegata'.** Similar to the above with its deep-green leaves heavily variegated with cream.

P. orba (Princess Astrid). A small compact and dense variety, with deep green leaves which are grey beneath and on grey stems.

P. 'Pink Lady'. This small variety has the rounded pale green leaves flushed pink, ageing to cream.

P. prostrata (Colombia). The small blue-green leaves are marked with silver, and hang on thread-like stems.

P. puteolata (Peru). A pretty, hanging variety, with narrow deep-green leaves, having five parallel yellowish stripes.

P. reflexa (Australia). Small grey-green leaves with sunken veins on upright stems.

Peperomia puteolata, Parallel Peperomia

Peperomia obtusifolia 'Alba'

Peperomia obtusifolia 'Royal Gold'

Peperomia obtusifolia 'Variegata'

Peperomia reflexa

Peperomia orba (Princess Astrid)

Peperomia prostrata

Peperomia 'Pink Lady'

180

Peperomia resedaeflora

Peperomia trinervis

P. resedaeflora. A flattish low growing plant, with grooved bright green leaves.

P. scandens 'Variegata'. A creeping or trailing plant with reddish stems, and heart shaped leaves, with milky green blotches, and cream edging.

P. sandersii (Brazil). Watermelon Begonia. A handsome small plant with round to pointed bluish-green leaves with showy bands of silver, pale beneath; reddish stems.

P. sarcophylla* (Ecuador, Colombia). A heavy plant, with large, broadly lanceolate, pendant, deep-green leaves, with a band of grey along the ribs; stems blotched red.

P. trinervis (S. America). Slender, upright variety with deep reddish-green leaves, each with three indented stripes, on red stems.

P. velutina* (Ecuador). Small branching variety, with red stems and small bronzy-green leaves, with pale green midrib and parallel veins.

P. verschaffelti* (Brazil). A beautiful variety with heart-shaped bluish-green leaves with broad silver bands between the veins.

P. viridis* (Mexico). An upright variety with thick heart-shaped vivid-green leaves.

PIPER   Piperaceae
Ornamental Peppers

Pipers are warmth-loving members of the same family as the Peperomias and are cared for similarly.

Varieties include:

P. crocatum (Peru). The colourful heart-shaped leaves are veined in pink, with purple reverse; a creeper.

P. magnificum (Peru). Lacquered Pepper Tree. Branching plant, resembling a Peperomia, with quilted, metallic-green leaves, marked ivory, and wine-red beneath.

Peperomia sandersii, Watermelon Begonia

Piper crocatum, Ornamental Pepper

Peperomia scandens 'Variegata', Philodendron Peperomia

Piper magnificum, Lacquered Pepper Tree

PERILEPTA (STROBILANTHES)   Acanthaceae

Persian Shield

P. dyerianus (Burma). This eye-catching purple and silver plant bears violet flowers. During warmer summer months it is a rapid grower, and should be regularly nipped to be kept bushy.

Grow: In a glasshouse or warm summer bush-house.
Position indoors: Requires very bright light to retain its colour. Adds brightness to a lit terrarium, but soon out-grows it.
Water: Keep moist.
Soil: Indoor Potting Mix.
Fertiliser: Complete Plant Food (dry, liquid, or foliar) monthly during summer.
Propagation: Easily grown from the small cuttings taken when nipping plant back for compactness.
Pests and problems: Generally observe.

PERISTROPHE   Acanthaceae

Marble Leaf

P. hyssopifolia 'Aureo-variegata' (Java). A small clustering plant, very attractive, with its bright yellow, variegated foliage, and small rose-pink flowers. Often sold as a pot plant for indoor growing, and too attractive to pass by.

Grow: Best grown in greenhouse.
Position indoors: Best near a bright, airy window or in a sunroom. Also good in a lit terrarium.
Water: Keep moist, occasionally spraying foliage.
Soil: General Potting Mix.
Fertiliser: Complete Plant Food sparingly, or foliar fertilisers every 3–4 weeks.
Pests and problems: Generally observe and remove to greenhouse at first signs of distress.

Perilepta (Strobilanthes) dyerianus, Persian Shield

Peristrophe hyssopifolia 'Aureo-variegata', Marble Leaf

PHILODENDRON   Araceae

This is a most versatile and hardy indoor plant, tolerating even the worst of indoor positions but thriving anywhere the light is good. The climbers are best grown on totems, where they can attach their aerial roots for added nourishment, resulting in larger leaf size, and better health. Philodendrons may also be grown in containers of water, if preferred. There are also dwarf or bushy types (known as self-heading), which do not require support. The leaves of these (particularly *selloum* types), if well back from the light source in a room, turn and stretch towards it. They should be regularly turned, and if they become misshapen the leaves can be tied to a plant ladder, making them more attractive and extending their indoor life. Self-heading Philodendrons are also hardy outdoors, tolerating quite cool winter temperatures.

Grow: In glasshouse or warm summer bush-house, in filtered sunlight.

Position indoors: Prefers strong light indoors or sunroom, but will tolerate poorer light for limited periods.

Water: Keep moist. If on a totem, concentrate the watering there, instead of the soil, to keep moist.

Soil: Indoor Potting Mix.

Fertiliser: Complete Plant Food (dry, liquid, or foliar) monthly during growth period, or foliar fertiliser to the leaves, if on a totem.

Propagation: Many are available from seeds, which have to be very fresh. Trailing varieties may be struck from cuttings, and very large and lanky self-headers may be topped.

Pests and problems: Scale insects and general observation.

Varieties include:

P. **'Andersons Red'.*** Similar to 'Red Wings', with stiff deep green leaves, on deep red stems, but differs by having a more rounded flower spathe.

P. andreanum (Colombia). A beautiful climber with large, oblong, velvety, iridescent, dark-olive leaves suffused with copper, and vivid ivory-white veins.

P. **'Angra dos Reis'** (Brazil). A slow creeper with very highly glossed arrow leaves on red-spotted stems.

P. bipinnatifidum (S. America). Self-heading, and each leaf having 10-12 segments each side.

P. cannifolium (Guyana). A low-creeping species, with narrow tapering, fresh-green leaves on swollen pale-green leaf-stalks.

P. costa rica. A creeping species; the oblong, pointed green leaves are red beneath.

Philodendron andreanum, Velour Philodendron

Philodendron 'Angra dos Reis'

Philodendron bipinnatifidum

Philodendron cannifolium, Flask Philodendron

Philodendron costa rica

PHILODENDRON, continued

P. crassinervium (Brazil). A creeper, with long, narrow, glossy, olive-green leaves, their thick midrib spotted in red.

P. cruentum* (Ecuador, Peru). An upright creeper, with oblong pointed green leaves; underside of leaf wine-red.

P. distantilobum (Amazon). Unusual, with the leaves very segmented.

P. domesticum (hastatum) (Brazil). A climber with fresh-green arrow-shaped leaves with paler veins.

***P. domesticum* 'Variegatum'.** In this form the fresh-green leaves are irregularly variegated with cream and yellow.

P. elegans (Trop. S. America). A high climber, with large deep-green deeply segmented finger-like leaves.

Philodendron domesticum (hastatum)

Philodendron domesticum 'Variegatum'

Philodendron elegans   *Philodendron crassinervium*

Philodendron distantilobum

P. erubescens* (Colombia). A climber with 25-cm arrow-shaped bronzy-green leaves edged with red, and red beneath.

P. × evansii (*selloum* cross). Self-heading variety, with beautiful long, segmented leaves, heavy texture and glossy.

P. fenzlii (Mexico, Costa Rica). A climber with thin, leathery, glossy, trilobed green leaves; segments broaden.

P. 'Florida' (*laciniatum × squamiferum*). A climbing variety with five-lobed deep-green leaves on slightly hairy stems.

P. 'Florida Variegata'. The deep green leaves are irregularly marked or mottled, sometimes fully, creamy-white.

P. giganteum (Puerto Rico to Trinidad). Beautiful variety with the young leaf of soft-textured bronze-green.

Philodendron fenzlii

Philodendron 'Florida Variegata'

Philodendron × evansii

Philodendron 'Florida'

Philodendron giganteum

PHILODENDRON, continued

*P. gloriosum** (Colombia). A slow creeper with heart-shaped satiny silver-green and pinkish leaves, with white veins and reddish margin.

P. 'Golden Erubescens'. The leaves are golden yellow, ageing to greenish yellow, but new growth is pinkish.

P. 'Golden Pride'. The cordatum type leaves are golden yellow, greenish with age or poor light. New introduction.

P. ilesmannii (Brazil). The long, heart-shaped, almost entirely white, leaves are marbled with grey and dark green.

*P. imbe** (Brazil). A climber with oblong to arrow-shaped deep-green leaves, some red beneath.

P. 'Jet Streak' (Colombia). The well-textured deep green leaves have white vein-markings.

*P. lacerum** (W. Indies). A climber with oval waxy-edged light-green leaves with paler veins.

*P. laciniatum** (Peru). A climber with oddly-shaped five-lobed leaves and elevated pale-green centre-markings.

Philodendron 'Golden Erubescens'

Philodendron 'Jet Streak'

Philodendron 'Golden Pride'

Philodendron ilesmannii

Philodendron lundii 'Sao Paulo'

186

Philodendron micans

P. lundii **'Sao Paulo'** (Sao Paulo). This variety will stand more sun and more cold. Self-heading.

P. mamei (Ecuador). A creeper with large broad arrow-shaped green leaves, and silvery-grey markings.

P. melanochrysum* (Colombia, Costa Rica). Black Gold. Almost black, velvety leaves, suffused with pink; similar to, but smaller than, *andreanum*.

P. melinonii* (Guyana). This dwarf species has a rosette, resembling a bird's nest, of shapely brownish-green leaves, on swollen reddish-brown leaf-stalks.

P. micans (Central America). A climber with small heart-shaped silky bronze leaves, reddish beneath.

P. **'New Yorker'**. A climber with highly glossed bright-green arrow-shaped leaves.

P. oxycardium (cordatum) (Central America). Best known of all Philodendron species; a tall climbing plant with deep-green heart-shaped leaves.

P. oxycardium **'Variegatum'**. Similar to the above with its heart-shaped leaves marbled with ivory white and grey-green.

Philodendron oxycardium (cordatum), Heartleaf Philodendron

Philodendron mamei, Quilted Silver-leaf

Philodendron 'New Yorker'

Philodendron oxycardium 'Variegatum' (cordatum 'Variegatum')

PHILODENDRON, continued

P. 'Painted Lady'. New foliage is gold, mottling green as it ages, on red stems. Newly introduced.

P. panduraeforme (Brazil). A climber with unusual fiddle-shaped fresh-green glossy leaves.

P. pertussum (Mexico). Miniature Monstera. A fast-climbing species which resembles *Monstera deliciosa*, only in miniature form.

P. pertussum 'Variegatum'. The variegated form, irregularly variegated with cream and yellow.

P. pittieri (Costa Rica). A slow climber with broad heart-shaped green leaves.

P. radiatum* (Mexico). Dubium. Creeper with broad rich-green leaves, which become more deeply lobed.

Philodendron pertussum 'Variegatum'

Philodendron 'Painted Lady'

Philodendron panduraeforme,
Fiddle Leaf Philodendron

Philodendron pertussum, Miniature
Monstera

Philodendron pittieri (microstictum)

188

P. radiatum × florida. A climbing variety with large deep-green unusually lobed leaves; vigorous.

P. 'Red Wings'. A creeper; its green, arrow-shaped leaves are red beneath, turning an attractive glossy wine-red. Shorter nodes. Flowers freely.

P. rubrum. Similar to 'Red Wings' and 'Andersons Red', but better suited for commercial growing. New leaves are red, greening with age.

P. 'Santa Leopoldina'. (Espirito Santo). A beautiful specie, with the highly glossed deep green leaf having a prominent ivory mid-rib; red flower spathe.

P. selloum (Brazil). Self-heading or non-climbing species, with large, attractively lobed, deep-green leaves. Will stand full sunlight and wide temperature variation.

Philodendron selloum, Lacy Tree Philodendron

Philodendron 'Red Wings'

Philodendron radiatum × florida

Philodendron rubrum

Philodendron 'Santa Leopoldina'

189

PHILODENDRON, continued

*P. sellowianum** (Brazil). Self-header with more deeply cut leaves than *selloum*.

P. sodiroi (Brazil). A creeper with smallish heart-shaped bluish-green leaves marked with silver, on red stems.

*P. squamiferum** (Guyana). A creeper with unusual five-lobed deep-green leaves and stems covered with red bristles.

P. squamiferum **'Variegatum'**. This handsome variety is faintly and irregularly variegated yellow.

*P. trifoliatum** (Venezuela). A climber with dark-green trilobed leaves, with a red spot at base of leaf, and depressed veins.

P. tuxla. A sturdy green-leafed variety, very suitable for commercial growing.

*P. tuxla × mahogany**. Has arrow-shaped leaves of deep green on pink stems, pinkish-fawn when young; slow climbing.

P. variifolium (Peru). A small, slow climber, with bluish-green (greenish-brown when young) heart-shaped leaves with silver markings.

P. verrucosum (Costa Rica). A climber with heart-shaped leaves of an iridescent velvety dark bronzy-green, with pale-green veins and edging of deep green, purplish beneath. Stems hairy.

P. wendlandii (Costa Rica, Panama). A bushy variety, arranged like a bird's nest, with its long narrow-oval waxy-green leaves on short, swollen round stems.

*P. williamsii** (Brazil). A self-heading variety with smooth, attractive, deep-green, long, arrow-shaped leaves which are wavy at the edges.

Philodendron squamiferum 'Variegatum'

Philodendron wendlandii, Bird's Nest Philodendron

Philodendron tuxla

Philodendron sodiroi, Silver Leaf Philodendron

Philodendron variifolium

Philodendron verrucosum, Velvet Leaf

190

PHORMIUM   Liliaceae

New Zealand Flax

Widely grown as specimen plants in gardens, and in pots on patios, and for limited periods indoors.

Position indoors: Requires an airy, well-lit, even sunny position. Take outdoors at first sign of distress.
Water: Keep moist.
Soil: General Potting Mix.
Fertiliser: Complete Plant Food (dry, liquid, or foliar) every 1–2 months.
Propagation: By division.
Pests and problems: Watch for mealy bug and scale.

Varieties include:
P. tenax **'Marginata'** (New Zealand). Variegated Flax. A clumping plant, with flat, green spreading leaves boldly edged in yellow.
P. tenax **'Variegatum'** (New Zealand). Variegated Flax. The green leaves are striped and margined with cream and yellow.

Phormium tenax 'Variegatum', New Zealand Variegated Flax

Phormium tenax 'Marginata', New Zealand Variegated Flax

PILEA Urticaceae

Friendship Plants

Another popular, small, house plant, suitable for hangers, terrariums, and specimen table pots. Many varieties may be grown in the garden, in tropical and temperate areas. Filtered sun.

Grow: In glasshouse, bush-house, or sheltered verandahs.
Position indoors: Sunroom, or near bright window, or lit terrarium.
Water: Moist, but not over-wet.
Soil: Indoor Potting Mix.
Fertiliser: Complete Plant Food every 1–2 months or foliar fertiliser every 2–4 weeks.
Propagation: Easy from cuttings.
Pests and problems: General observation. Pinch back regularly, to keep compact.

Varieties include:
P. cadieri (Indo-China). Aluminium Plant. A rapid-growing small plant with bright green glossy leaves with silver bubble markings and edgings; tiny white stem flowers.
P. cadieri **'Minima'**. A dwarf species of the above with smaller, quilted, olive-green leaves with silver bubble markings.

Pilea cadieri, Aluminium Plant

Pilea cadieri 'Minima', Dwarf Aluminium Plant

Pilea microphylla, 'Rubrum', Red Military Fern

Pilea involucrata, Friendship Plant

Pilea microphylla, Artillery Plant or Military Fern

P. involucrata (Peru). Friendship Plant. A densely branching small plant with quilted brown and deep-green leaves, reddish beneath; unusual tiny rosy-red flower-head.

P. microphylla (West Indies). Artillery Plant or Military Fern. A small, densely branched, succulent green plant resembling a fern; small leaves.

P. microphylla 'Rubrum'. Similar to the above only with its green foliage turning to and flushed with wine-red; requires sun to colour properly.

P. microphylla 'Variegata'. Low-growing, with cream variegation.

P. 'Moon Valley' (Costa Rica). An unusual small plant, with hairy, quilted leaves, green at the edges and overlaid coppery-brown to black; greenish-white flower heads.

P. nummulariifolia (W. Indies to Peru). Creeping Charlie. A thickly creeping variety with numerous fresh-green leaves. Suits basket.

P. 'Silver Tree' (Syn. 'Silver and Bronze') (Caribbean). A small branching plant with bronze-green oval leaves with a broad centre-band of silver.

P. spruceana 'Norfolk'. An attractive variety with the newer leaves reddish-bronze, shading to mature leaves of blackish-green and silver.

P. spruceana 'Curly Top'. Similar to the above, but the younger leaves are curled.

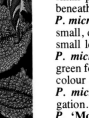

Pilea 'Moon Valley'

Pilea spruceana 'Norfolk'

Pilea microphylla 'Variegata',
Variegated Military Fern

Pilea 'Silver Tree'

Pilea spruceana 'Curly Top'

Pilea nummulariifolia, Creeping Charlie

193

PLECTRANTHUS   Labiatae

Swedish Ivy

Swedish Ivies are fast-growing plants, and because of their spreading growth and hanging foliage are suitable indoors for baskets and pots in macrame hangers. In the garden they are a hardy form of groundcover.

Grow: Prefer filtered light, outdoors.
Position indoors: Require good light to filtered sun.
Water: Keep moist.
Soil: General Potting Mix.
Fertiliser: Occasional fertilising with Complete Plant Food, alternated with foliar feeding.
Propagation: From cuttings.
Pests and problems: Fairly trouble-free.

Varieties include:
P. nummularis (australis) (Australia, Pacific Islands). Has spreading stems of green leaves and white flowers.
P. oertendahlii (Natal). Has blue-green leaves veined in white, purple beneath; pink flowers.

PORTULACARIA   Portulacaceae

Jade Plant

P. afra (S. Africa). Jade Plant or Elephant Bush. This hardy heat-tolerant plant may be grown in most of those tough outdoor positions, such as against brick-work in hot sun, or neglected in pots on verandahs, and still survive. However, given better treatment, it also gives better appearance. It stands up to hot window sills, indoors, and is well worth a try. There is also a variegated form.

Grow: Outdoors, anywhere.
Position indoors: Any airy, brightly-lit, or sunny position indoors, or sunroom.
Water: Thoroughly water (immerse pot is best) then allow to dry before repeating.
Soil: General Potting Mix.
Fertiliser: Complete Plant Food (dry, liquid, or foliar) every 2–3 months.
Propagation: Takes root easily, from cutting.
Pests and problems: General observation.

Plectranthus nummularis (australis), Swedish Ivy

Plectranthus oertendahlii, Prostrate Coleus

Portulacaria afra

PRIMULA   Primulaceae

Primroses

Primula varieties may be annual or perennial, and are usually grown in Australia for garden displays. However, both may be used as potted plants for indoor decoration. The annual varieties should be discarded when the display has finished, but the perennial ones are kept, or planted in a sheltered garden corner until the following autumn, when they may be divided and repotted for the next season's growing. Primulas are very colourful.

Grow: Start in bush-house, and grow there till flowering commences.
Position indoors: Bring indoors when flowering. They need a brightly lit, airy window position, but no sun through the glass.
Water: Keep evenly moist, empty surplus from saucer.
Soil: General Potting Mix.
Fertiliser: Complete Plant Food (dry, liquid, or foliar) monthly, or foliar fertiliser every 2 weeks until dormancy.
Propagation: Annuals, from seed. Perennials are from seed, or division at dormancy.
Pests and problems: Carefully observe.

Varieties include:

Annual
P. malacoides (Yunnan, China). A winter–spring flowering annual with small light-green hairy leaves, and many heads of flowers. Many new and larger flowering varieties are available for pot culture.

Perennial
P. obconica (China). A winter- to spring-blooming pot plant with broad green hairy leaves and showy heads of large flowers in colours from blue to pink and red. Good for indoor decoration.
P. polyantha Polyanthus. A spring-flowering perennial with narrow crinkled leaves and bearing heads of flowers in many colours (yellow, orange, bronze, maroon), often with white eyes.
P. sinensis (China). Similar to the above, with hairy foliage and heads of large fringed flowers in many colours.

Primula malacoides, Fairy Primrose (annual)

Primula polyantha, Pacific Giant Polyanthus

Primula obconica

Primula sinensis, Chinese Primrose

195

RHOEO   Commelinaceae

Moses in the Cradle

Tiny white flowers clustered inside purple boat-shaped bracts have given this plant its common name.

Grow: In tropical and subtropical gardens, or in greenhouses or glasshouses and warm summer bush-houses elsewhere. Prefers filtered sun.
Position indoors: Sunroom or near bright, airy window indoors, or any sheltered, airy position around the outside of the house.
Water: Keep moist, but not over-wet.
Soil: General Potting Mix.
Fertiliser: Complete Plant Food (dry, liquid, or foliar) monthly.
Propagation: From sizeable cuttings, or division.
Pests and problems: General observation.

Varieties include:
R. spathacea (discolor) (Mexico). This stiff, brittle plant is deep green on top of the leaf, and purple beneath. The purple boat-shaped bracts have white flowers peeping out.
R. spathacea **'Vittata'** *(discolour* **'Vittata').** A variegated form, with leaves striped pale yellow, tinted with red.

Rhoeo spathacea (discolour), Moses in the Cradle

RIBBON GRASSES

Chlorophytum, Liriope, and Ophiopogon

These fast-growing hardy plants are very adaptable. They are suitable for open garden positions, rockeries, and hanging pots for both outdoors and indoors. Commonly called Ribbon Grass, Spider Plant, or Lily Turf.

Grow: Any position from bright sun to good light.
Position indoors: Sunroom or any well-lit position. Ideal for hanging pots or macrame hangers. Also used as a filler plant around the base of tall and lanky plants.
Water: Keep evenly moist.
Soil: General Potting Mix.
Fertiliser: Complete Plant Food (dry, liquid, or foliar).
Propagation: By young plantlets from the runners or division.
Pests and problems: Scale and spider mites.

Varieties include:

CHLOROPHYTUM
Ribbon Grass, Spider Plant

C. bichetii (W. Africa). Smaller variety, forming bushy tufts.
C. comosum **'Picturatum'** (S. and Central Africa). Green leaves, with wide central yellow bands.
C. comosum **'Variegatum'** (Africa). Ribbon Grass. Rosettes of arching, fresh-green linear leaves, edged in creamy-white. The long flower racemes develop aerial-rooting plantlets.
C. comosum **'Vittatum'** (Africa). Spider Plant. A low, narrow-leafed plant, deep green with a white centre stripe. Plantlets develop from the long trailing racemes.

LIRIOPE
Lily Turf

L. muscari **'Variegata'** (Japan, China). Big Blue Lily Turf. Similar to Ophiopogon but with racemes of blue flowers.

OPHIOPOGON
Lily Turf

O. jaburan **'Variegatus'** (Japan). White Lily Turf. Long grass-like green leaves striped and edged with white; racemes of white flowers.

Chlorophytum bichetii, St Bernard's Lily

Rhoeo spathacea 'Vittata', Variegated Boat Lily

Ophiopogon jaburan 'Variegatus', White Turf Lily

Liriope muscari 'Variegata', Big Blue Turf Lily

Chlorophytum comosum 'Vittatum', Spider Plant – with runners

Chlorophytum comosum 'Variegatum', Variegated Ribbon Grass

SAINTPAULIA   Gesneriaceae

African Violets

African Violets are a most popular house plant. I know of no other plant which can spend its whole life indoors, producing its buds and flowering to perfection, year after year. The number of African Violet societies testifies to their popularity, and every flowering plant offered for sale is snapped up.

Culture: I consider Saintpaulias to be the easiest of house plants. Their main requirement is no sun, but very good light, as this helps keep them in flower. It is a matter of selecting the most favourable position. If there is too much sun, they will grow and flower but their leaves will be spoiled by sunburn. If set too far back from the window, they will still grow, but not flower.

During my life as a nurseryman I have heard of all sorts of successful ways of growing Saintpaulias. Most of these suggestions seem to conflict with each other and often with my own theories. If you have found a successful method of growing them, keep going with this. Otherwise, you may wish to try mine.

The summer temperatures within the average home are ideal. Winter temperatures can be a bit cool in some districts, so select a warmer room, if this is the case. Often it is much cooler next to the glass, so they may have to be moved back a little, until the temperatures pick up again.

Position indoors: Select either a southern window sill without curtains, or an eastern window with light curtains, to filter the morning sun, and prevent burning of the leaves. A northern window sill is all right in summer, but not in winter: lift the plant down until the sun has moved off this window sill. A western window is satisfactory if you pull the curtain or blind across while the sun is on that window. African Violets will flower well in any of these positions of full light. Watch closely and use common sense. The plants may be placed further back into the room from any of these positions if desired. However if they are growing happily, but not flowering, they will have to be moved closer to the bright light source. Remember the more light, the better they flower, but direct sun will burn and mark the leaves.

Water: As they love humidity, fill the saucers with pebbles and keep moist, but empty out any excess.

Soil: Indoor Potting Mix, or Special Saintpaulia Mix.

Fertiliser: Be careful not to use any fertiliser containing sulphate of ammonia. I prefer fish emulsion, but there are plenty of acceptable Complete Fertilisers available.

Propagation: A cut leaf with stem may be rooted in water. I prefer to strike these in a small pot of sphagnum moss. Older, leggy plants may be divided in spring, or after a prolonged flowering, before winter.

Pests and problems: Observe for spider mites and mealy bug.

Varieties include:
These days, with easy pollination, there are varieties of African Violets by the thousands, far too many to list here. Saintpaulia societies make some attempt at control by registering names submitted by their members, but often non-members turn up with ones named after each of their children, or with cross-variations. The accompanying illustrations show some of the most popular varieties available here.

Chlorophytum comosum 'Picturatum'

Saintpaulia 'Alaskan Waters'

Saintpaulia 'Alpine'

Saintpaulia 'Blue Boy'

Saintpaulia 'Apollo'

Saintpaulia 'Bold Design'

Saintpaulia 'Avis'

Saintpaulia 'Budd's Pink Waltz'

Saintpaulia 'Early Morn'

Saintpaulia 'Cloud 9'

Saintpaulia 'Fairy Skies'

Saintpaulia 'Glendon Pink'

Saintpaulia 'Fischer's Follies'

Saintpaulia 'Double Delight'

Saintpaulia 'Fischer's Mars'

199

Saintpaulia 'Grand Duke'

Saintpaulia 'Juliet'

Saintpaulia 'Ionic'

Saintpaulia 'Pagan Fire'

Saintpaulia 'New Star Pink'

Saintpaulia 'Plum Royal'

Saintpaulia 'Lullaby'

Saintpaulia 'Plum Tips Double'

Saintpaulia 'Prom Queen'

Saintpaulia 'Star Gaze'

Saintpaulia 'Rose Linda'

Saintpaulia 'Saturn'

Saintpaulia 'Snow Spirits'

Saintpaulia 'Red Comet'

Saintpaulia 'Showstopper'

Saintpaulia 'Sparkling Waters'

Saintpaulia 'Wedding Ring'

Saintpaulia 'Tinsel'

Saintpaulia 'Strike Me Pink'

Saintpaulia 'White Pride'

SANCHEZIA   Acanthaceae

S. nobilis (Ecuador). The young growth is strikingly marked with yellow veins, but tends to become green as it ages. Showy yellow flowers in red bracts.

Grow: Outdoors in tropics and subtropics, otherwise in glasshouse or warm summer bush-house.
Position indoors: Sunroom or near bright, airy window.
Water: Keep moist to wet.
Soil: General Potting Mix.
Fertiliser: Complete Plant Food (dry, liquid, or foliar) monthly.
Propagation: From cuttings.
Pests and problems: General observation.

Sanchezia nobilis

SANSEVIERIA   Liliaceae
Mother-in-Law's Tongue or Snake Plant

A very tough indoor plant, outlasting all others under the worst of conditions. I have three clustered pots of *S. trifasciata* 'Laurentii' in my home, which flower twice yearly, emitting the sweetest of perfume. I cannot understand why this plant is treated so disdainfully by many who seek a hardy indoor plant.

Grow: In tropical and subtropical gardens, or even warm temperate gardens, or as pot plants on patios and verandahs. Some varieties are more cold-tender, and require glasshouse conditions.
Position indoors: Best in positions adjacent to bright windows but will tolerate even the poorest of light, for short periods.
Water: Allow to dry out before re-watering.
Soil: General Potting Mix. Best to pot in earthenware pots as the strength of the new root suckers can push through, or even burst, plastic pots.
Fertiliser: Complete Plant Food, every 1–2 months, or use foliar fertiliser more regularly.
Propagation: The green varieties may be mass propagated from cutting and planting leaf sections of 8–10 cm. All are best grown by division. It is better to plant several in one pot, as they take years of growing to get the massed effect.
Pests and problems: None observed. Do not over-water.

Varieties include:
S. cylindrica (Africa). Round, arching, dark-green leaves to 1.5 m tapering to a point; pinkish flowers.

Sansevieria cylindrica, Spear Sansevieria

SANSEVIERIA, continued

S. guineensis 'Marginata'. The broad untidy leaf is heavily variegated with deep yellow.

S. intermedia (E. Trop. Africa). The short thick leaves are deep green, banded grey.

S. liberica (W. Africa). A striking variety with bold erect-growing thick leaves to 1 m tall, with broad bands of white either side of the bluish grey-green leaves.

S. parva (E. Africa). Forms a rosette of fresh green with deeper green cross-bands, on fast-running root.

S. 'Silver Sheen'. A low-growing variety, with the flat leaves silver-grey.

S. scabrifolia (S.E. Africa). Miniature to 15 cm, deep green leaves banded silver, with corky edges.

S. stuckyi (Zimbabwe). Similar to *cylindrica,* but with open leaf channels.

S. subscripta (S. Africa). Broader-leafed variety than *S. trifasciata* with its greyish to dark-green leaves edged brownish-red; flowers white.

S. trifasciata (Africa, India). Snake Plant. An erect plant with long, smooth, and glossy, tapering deep-green leaves to 1 m with paler cross-bands and white flowers.

S. trifasciata 'Bantels Sensation'. White sport of *'laurentii'* with variable colour marking.

S. trifasciata 'Hahnii'. A dwarf species, sporting from *laurentii,* and resembling a bird's nest, with a rosette of broad, smooth, dark-green leaves, with pale-green cross-bands.

S. trifasciata 'Golden Hahnii'. A handsome sport of Hahnii, with broad golden-yellow bands alongside the margins, and cross-banded in grey.

S. trifasciata 'Silver Hahnii'. A Hahnii sport, which is almost entirely metallic silver-grey; the occasional markings are deep green.

S. trifasciata 'Laurentii' (Congo). A very striking form of *trifasciata* with its deep-green leaves broadly edged in yellow.

S. trifasciata 'Laurentii Compacta' (Goldiana). More compact version of *laurentii,* with stiff, blackish-green leaves, having gold bands.

Sansevieria liberica

Sansevieria 'Silver Sheen'

Sansevieria scabrifolia, Miniature Sansevieria

Sansevieria stuckyi

Sansevieria guineensis 'Marginata', Variegated Bowstring Hemp

Sansevieria subscripta

Sansevieria parva

204   *Sansevieria intermedia*

Sansevieria trifasciata, Snake Plant or Mother-in-Law's Tongue

Sansevieria trifasciata 'Bantels Sensation', White Sansevieria

Sansevieria trifasciata 'Laurentii', Variegated Snake Plant

Sansevieria trifasciata 'Golden Hahnii'

Sansevieria trifasciata 'Hahnii', Bird's Nest

Sansevieria trifasciata 'Laurentii Compacta' (Goldiana)

Sansevieria trifasciata 'Silver Hahnii'

SAXIFRAGA   Saxifragaceae

Strawberry Begonia

Strawberry Begonias are so called because of their similarity to strawberries in sending out tendrils with plantlets that hang, and their Begonia-like leaves and flowers.

Grow: Saxifraga are best-suited to greenhouses, growing in hanging pots. Their massed growth and trailing habit is quite effective, particularly in summer, when they flower.

Position indoors: Sunroom, or near a bright or even filtered sunny and airy window. Also good in a lit terrarium. Best on sheltered patios.

Water: Allow to dry out between waterings.

Soil: General Potting Mix.

Fertiliser: Complete Plant Food (dry, liquid, or foliar) monthly during summer, or foliar fertiliser each 2–3 weeks.

Propagation: Grow the young plantlets, or divide a larger pot-full.

Pests and problems: Mealy bug. Observe regularly if indoors, and move out again at first sign of distress.

Varieties include:

S. stolonifera (China, Japan). Strawberry Begonia. A small plant with olive-green leaves, silver-grey veins and markings, purplish beneath; pinkish-white flowers. Produces thread-like runners with plantlets similar to strawberries.

S. stolonifera 'Tricolour'. Magic Carpet. An attractive smaller and more tender species of the above, with deep-green leaves, broadly marked with ivory-white and tinted pink and purplish beneath.

Saxifraga stolonifera, Strawberry Begonia

Saxifraga stolonifera 'Tricolour', Magic Carpet

205

SCHIZANTHUS　　Solanaceae

Poor Man's Orchid

S. wisetonensis (Chile). An annual flower, generally used for bedding in the garden, but wonderful when used in hanging pots on patios. It may also be grown in pots outdoors, and taken indoors when in flower, for special display.

SENECIO　　Compositae

German Ivy or Flowering Ivy

This succulent is often mistaken for Ivy. It can be grown as a garden creeper, where it flowers with yellow daisy-like blooms, or can be grown in pots or hanging baskets on patios, verandahs, or indoors.

Position indoors: Sunrooms, or near a sunny or brightly lit window.
Water: Allow to dry between waterings.
Soil: General Potting Mix.
Fertiliser: Complete Plant Food sparingly, monthly, or foliar fertiliser each 2–3 weeks.
Propagation: From cuttings.
Pests and problems: General observation.

Varieties include:
S. macroglossus (S. Africa). Creeper with succulent ivy-shaped leaves and yellow, daisy-like flowers.
S. macroglossus **'Variegatum'.** The cream, variegated form.

Schizanthus wisetonensis, Poor Man's Orchid

Senecio macroglossus, German Ivy

Senecio macroglossus 'Variegatum', Variegated German Ivy

SINNINGIA, SMITHIANA, and STREPTOCARPUS

SINNINGIA
Gesneriaceae

Gloxinia

These handsome, flowering pot plants require similar treatment to Tuberous Begonias. These days, there are many hybrid varieties offered, either as plants or, during winter, as corms. They range from the standard *speciosa* with bells of 5 cm, to *gigantea*, with bells of 7-10 cm, and there are also some double varieties now appearing. All are richly coloured or two-toned.

Grow: In glasshouses or warm, summer bush-houses.
Position indoors: Sunroom or near bright, airy window.
Water: Keep evenly moist, drying off as the plant enters the bulb stage.
Soil: Indoor Potting Mix.
Fertiliser: Complete Plant Food (dry, liquid, or foliar) monthly, until drying-off stage.
Propagation: From seed, or selected varieties may be grown by planting a leaf.
Pests and problems: General observation.

Varieties include:
S. grandiflora (Brazil). A tuberous plant, growing and flowering over the summer months, with soft furry leaves and upright bell-shaped flowers in various shadings from white to reds and blues.

Smithiana 'Orange King', Temple Bells

STREPTOCARPUS
Gesneriaceae

Cape Primrose

The flowers are similar to Gloxinias but smaller, and with a number to a stem. They are grown from seeds or leaf cuttings, or by division.

Grow: In cool glasshouse or bush-house, taking indoors when flowering. Directions similar to Gloxinias.

Varieties include:
Miniature hybrids ('Baby Doll', etc.) and 'Weismoor' hybrids in a variety of colours.

Sinningia grandiflora, Gloxinia

SMITHIANA
Gesneriaceae

Temple Bells

This very attractive plant has beautiful, large, velvety leaves overlaid with red and orange bell flowers, yellow inside, and spotted red.

Grow: In glasshouses, from seeds, leaves, or division of rhizomes. Cultural directions similar to Gloxinias.

Varieties include:
Orange King, Golden King, Rose Queen, and many cultivated hybrids.

Streptocarpus 'Baby Doll', miniature Cape Primrose

Streptocarpus 'Weismoor', hybrid Cape Primrose

CHIRITA   Gesneriaceae

Silver Chirita

As this is another member of the same group of plants as Gloxinia the growing conditions are the same.

Varieties include:
C. sinensis (S. China). Stemless plant, 15 cm high, with attractive green and silver variegated leaves, and lilac Gloxinia-like flowers.

Chirita sinensis, Silver Chirita

KOHLERIA   Gesneriaceae

Tree Gloxinia

K. eriantha (Colombia). A hardy plant for pot or sheltered rockery garden, with dull, hairy, deep green leaves, maroon beneath, and orange trumpet flowers. Refer to Gloxinias for cultural directions.

Kohleria eriantha, Tree Gloxinia

SOLEIROLIA   Urticaceae
(HELIXINE)

Baby's Tears

S. soleirolii (Corsica). Baby's Tears. This low, dense, creeping plant has minute green leaves.

Position indoors: Warm, brightly-lit rooms, terrariums or sunrooms. Suitable for hanging pots.
Water: Keep moist, preferably hose foliage weekly.
Soil: Indoor Potting Mix.
Fertiliser: Use a foliar fertiliser every 3–4 weeks.
Propagation: Divide plant.
Pests and problems: General observation.

Soleirolia (Helixine) soleirolii, Baby Tears

SONERILA   Melastomaceae

Pearly Sonerila

S. margaritacea 'Argentea' (Java). This attractive, small plant has olive-green leaves, overlaid with silver, and pink flowers. As the plant requires tropical warmth, with high humidity, it should be grown in a glasshouse.

Position indoors: If you wish to try it indoors, select a bright, warm, and well-lit position, and place the pot on a saucer of pebbles to provide humidity. If you have one, a lit terrarium may be more suitable.

Water: Allow to dry before re-watering. Keep pebbles in saucer moist.

Soil: Indoor Potting Mix.

Fertiliser: Use fish emulsion or foliar fertiliser, monthly.

Propagation: From cuttings.

Pests and problems: Carefully observe.

Sonerila margaritacea 'Argentea', Pearly Sonerila

SPATHIPHYLLUM   Araceae

Peace Lily, Madonna Lily

Spathiphyllums are very hardy as indoor plants. They are almost as tough as their relatives, Philodendrons, but also have the added advantage of bearing white, lily-white flowers which last for many weeks. Flowers turn green with age.

Grow: In glasshouse or warm summer bush-house, or under trees in tropical gardens.

Position indoors: Best in any well-lit position but will tolerate poorer light for short periods. However, this affects the flowering.

Water: Keep moist, not over-wet. These are thirsty plants, therefore immerse pots until bubbling ceases.

Soil: General Potting Mix.

Fertiliser: Complete Plant Food (dry, liquid, or foliar) monthly, or fish emulsion, which seems to help with flowering.

Propagation: From seed, or divide clustered plants, remembering a flower comes from each major leaf stem.

Pests and problems: Watch for slugs and snails.

Varieties include:
S. 'Clevelandii'*. A tall variety, to 1 m, with narrow deep green leaves, forming a flower from each leaf joint during the season.
S. 'Mauna Loa'. A cross from 'Clevelandii', with broader and more handsome leaves.
S. 'Tasson'. A later introduction, similar to 'Mauna Loa', but more evenly compact and free flowering.
S. wallisii (Colombia, Venezuela). A smaller variety, seasonally producing many flowers at the one time.

Spathiphyllum wallisii, Dwarf Madonna Lily

Spathiphyllum 'Mauna Loa', Madonna Lily

Spathiphyllum 'Tasson', Madonna Lily

SYNGONIUM   Araceae

Nephthytis

This fast-growing trailer, a close relative to Philodendrons, is extremely hardy indoors. Previously, all plants purchased used to be grown from cuttings, and became rather lengthy. Now, with tissue-culture propagation, they develop into much nicer compact plants, adding to their popularity. They are ideal for hanging pots, and if kept nipped back will remain bushy.

Grow: In glasshouse for best results.
Position indoors: Prefers good light for best results, but will tolerate less light for short periods.
Water: Keep moist.
Soil: General Potting Mix.
Fertiliser: Complete Plant Food or foliar fertiliser, monthly.
Propagation: From cuttings.
Pests and problems: Generally observe.

Varieties include:
S. **'Frostie'.** A beautiful climber, resembling a Philodendron, with rounded heart-shaped green leaves heavily sprayed with white.
S. macrophylla (Mexico to Panama). Big Leaf Syngonium. Eventually splits into segments similar to an Umbrella Tree leaf.
*S. podophyllum** (Central America). Nephthytis. A climber with deep-green, fine, arrow-shaped leaves in juvenile stage.
S. podophyllum **'Albolineatum'.** (Mexico, Nicaragua). A climber with trilobed leaves, with silver-white centre-markings; mature leaves are green.
S. podophyllum **'Green Gold'** (Mexico). The arrow-shaped juvenile green leaves are suffused and marbled with yellowish-green.
S. podophyllum **'Imperial White'.** The juvenile arrow-shaped leaves are greenish-white, with a narrow green border. Remains compact longer than other varieties.
S. podophyllum **'Noack'.** This popular commercially-sold variety is both handsome and compact due to tissue-culture, but eventually lengthens out.

Syngonium podophyllum 'Green Gold'

Syngonium podophyllum 'Imperial White'

Syngonium 'Frostie'

Syngonium macrophylla, Big Leaf Syngonium

Syngonium podophyllum 'Albolineatum', Arrowhead Vine

210

S. podophyllum 'White Butterfly'. Also from tissue culture, all white, but needs strong light to stay white, greening in poorer light.

S. podophyllum 'White Butterfly' variant. This sport is also being grown commercially. The narrow leaf is effective.

S. podophyllum 'Variegata', (or 'Fantasy'). Newly introduced with contrasting pure white variegation. Needs good light.

TOLMIEA   Saxifragaceae
Piggy-back Plant

T. menziesii (N.W. North America). Called the Piggy-back Plant because small plantlets develop from the centre of each leaf.

Grow: In warm summer bush-house or glasshouse.
Position indoors: Sunroom or near brightly lit and airy window.
Water: Keep moist, not over-wet.
Soil: General Potting Mix.
Fertiliser: Complete Plant Food monthly or foliar fertiliser at half-strength every 2–3 weeks.
Propagation: Cut and plant a matured leaf, with plantlets to the base of the leaf; it will soon grow.
Pests and problems: Watch for mealy bug.

Syngonium podophyllum 'White Butterfly' variant

Syngonium podophyllum 'Variegata', Fantasy

Syngonium podophyllum 'Noack'

Syngonium podophyllum 'White Butterfly'

Tolmiea menziesii, Piggy-back Plant

211

WANDERING JEWS   Commelinaceae

These members of the *Commelinaceae* family are useful outdoors as ground covers. They are also grown indoors in hanging baskets and pots, around the tops of other pot plants, or in terrariums. They may be cut and grown in water alone. I have found it preferable, as with Ivy, to grow the plants outdoors, then to pick and grow the cuttings indoors, in fancy pots of water. When desired, or if they become too large, they may be potted-up into soil, and become nice spill-over plants for a patio table.

Grow: In shaded and sheltered positions, preferably where they will receive plenty of water.
Position indoors: Medium to bright light. Cuttings in water seem to tolerate less light for longer periods.
Water: In soil, allow surface soil to dry between waterings. In water, use a knob of charcoal and change as required to keep fresh.
Soil: General Potting Mix.
Fertiliser: A few granules of Complete Plant Food, monthly, or use foliar fertilisers every few weeks.
Propagation: From cuttings in sand or water.
Pests and problems: General observation.

Varieties include:

SETCREASEA

S. purpurea **'Purple Heart'** (Mexico). A brittle plant with narrow hairy bright-purple leaves in sunlight; pink three-petalled flowers.
S. striata (Callisia elegans) (S. Mexico). A succulent creeper with smallish olive-green leaves, with parallel white stripes; purple beneath; white flowers.

SIDERASIS

S. fuscata (Tradescantia pyrrheima) (Brazil). A low clustering plant, with a rosette of oblong olive-green leaves, with a silver centre stripe, and covered in brown hairs; lavender-blue flowers in base.

Siderasis fuscata, Brown Spiderwort

TRADESCANTIA

T. albiflora albo-vittata* (Central America). A large-leafed branching species, with fleshy green leaves, striped and bordered in white; white flowers.
T. blossfeldiana (Brazil). A strong, branching species with olive-green leaves, purple beneath, and silvery hairs; flowers white, tipped with purple.
T. blossfeldiana **'Variegata'.** A very attractive form, with the bronzy-green leaves variegated cream, which turns mauve-pink.
T. fluminensis **'Variegata'*** (Argentina, Brazil). A trailer with smaller, shining, fresh-green leaves, striped in yellow and cream; flowers white.
T. laekensis **'Rainbow'*.** A trailer with small green leaves, with white stripes tinted with pinkish purple; white flowers.
T. sillamontana (pexata) (S. Africa). White Velvet. A succulent little creeper with pale-green leaves covered with soft white hairs; orchid-pink flowers.

Setcreasia purpurea, Purple Heart

Setcreasea striata (Callisia elegans)

Tradescantia sillamontana (pexata), White Velvet

ZEBRINA

Z. pendula (Mexico). Wandering Jew. A trailer with deep-green to purple leaves with two broad glistening, silver stripes, purple beneath; flowers are rosy-purple.

Z. pendula 'Quadricolor'. A very colourful form with purplish-green leaves, banded with glistening white, and with pink, red, and silver stripes; edging and underside of leaf purple. A pretty but more delicate variety.

Z. purpusii (Mexico). A trailer with fleshy brittle olive to purple leaves with faint, green stripes; vivid purple beneath; lavender flowers.

Tradescantia blossfeldiana 'Variegata'

Zebrina pendula, Silver Wandering Jew

Zebrina pendula 'Quadricolour', Happy Wandering Jew

Tradescantia blossfeldiana

Zebrina purpusii, Red Wandering Jew

213

VINCA   Apocynaceae

Band Plant

V. major 'Variegata' (Europe, N. Africa). This small, twining creeper is very attractive as a rockery plant in sheltered areas, or as a patio pot or basket plant, but will only last for short periods indoors. It bears attractive blue flowers.

Position indoors: Select a bright to sunny window, but move outdoors at first sign of distress. Prune back the trails to keep bushy.
Water: Moist but not over-wet.
Soil: General Potting Mix.
Fertiliser: Complete Plant Food (dry, liquid, or foliar) monthly.
Propagation: From cutting or plantlets where tendrils take root.
Pests and problems: None observed.

XANTHOSOMA   Araceae

X. lindenii '**Magnificum**' (Colombia). A very striking relative of Philodendrons, best grown in humid glasshouse conditions, such as under benches, where it can take root and run at will, or on sphagnum moss-covered poles. If taken indoors, I would suggest a lit terrarium, with a sphagnum moss floor covering, fairly bright light, and a warm position. Fertilise monthly with foliar fertiliser.

Vinca major 'Variegata', Band Plant

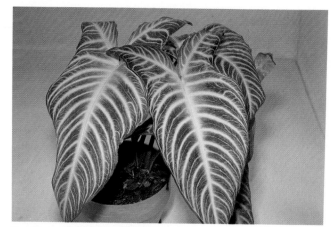

Xanthosma lindenii 'Magnificum', Indian Kale

214

ZEBRINA

Z. pendula (Mexico). Wandering Jew. A trailer with deep-green to purple leaves with two broad glistening, silver stripes, purple beneath; flowers are rosy-purple.

***Z. pendula* 'Quadricolor'.** A very colourful form with purplish-green leaves, banded with glistening white, and with pink, red, and silver stripes; edging and underside of leaf purple. A pretty but more delicate variety.

Z. purpusii (Mexico). A trailer with fleshy brittle olive to purple leaves with faint, green stripes; vivid purple beneath; lavender flowers.

Tradescantia blossfeldiana 'Variegata'

Zebrina pendula, Silver Wandering Jew

Zebrina pendula 'Quadricolour', Happy Wandering Jew

Tradescantia blossfeldiana

Zebrina purpusii, Red Wandering Jew

213

VINCA Apocynaceae

Band Plant

V. major 'Variegata' (Europe, N. Africa). This small, twining creeper is very attractive as a rockery plant in sheltered areas, or as a patio pot or basket plant, but will only last for short periods indoors. It bears attractive blue flowers.

Position indoors: Select a bright to sunny window, but move outdoors at first sign of distress. Prune back the trails to keep bushy.
Water: Moist but not over-wet.
Soil: General Potting Mix.
Fertiliser: Complete Plant Food (dry, liquid, or foliar) monthly.
Propagation: From cutting or plantlets where tendrils take root.
Pests and problems: None observed.

XANTHOSOMA Araceae

X. lindenii '**Magnificum**' (Colombia). A very striking relative of Philodendrons, best grown in humid glasshouse conditions, such as under benches, where it can take root and run at will, or on sphagnum moss-covered poles. If taken indoors, I would suggest a lit terrarium, with a sphagnum moss floor covering, fairly bright light, and a warm position. Fertilise monthly with foliar fertiliser.

Vinca major 'Variegata', Band Plant

Xanthosma lindenii 'Magnificum', Indian Kale

214

ACKNOWLEDGMENTS

To my wife Eileen, whose love and assistance with the text
made this book and the previous ones possible.
My thanks for assistance with material goes to Len Dellow,
Ian Raward, Neville and Pat Raward, Olwen Ferris, and my
son Gary who is as ardent an enthusiast as myself; also to
the W.O.N.S. nurserymen for use of their registered trade
names.
My special thanks also to all the unnamed friends who have
assisted me in their unrecognised way to produce this book.
Finally I thank Mike Page, now retired from Rigby Pub-
lishers, for his timeless efforts and faith in this venture.